APPLE, TREE

# Apple, Tree

## WRITERS ON THEIR PARENTS

*Edited and with an introduction by Lise Funderburg*

UNIVERSITY OF NEBRASKA PRESS    LINCOLN

Frontispiece: *N⁰ 127 Fruitless*, © Tanya Marcuse, www.tanyamarcuse.com

Library of Congress Cataloging-in-Publication Data
Names: Funderburg, Lise, author.
Title: Apple, tree: writers on their parents / edited and
    with an introduction by Lise Funderburg.
Other titles: Writers on their parents
Description: Lincoln: University of Nebraska Press, 2019.
Identifiers: LCCN 2019005313
    ISBN 9781496212092 (cloth: alk. paper)
    ISBN 9781496217219 (epub)
    ISBN 9781496217226 (mobi)
    ISBN 9781496217233 (pdf)
Subjects: LCSH: Authors, American—Family relationships. |
    Parent and child—United States. | Parenting—Psychological
    aspects—United States. | Identity (Psychology)—United
    States. | Self. | Authors, American—Biography.
Classification: LCC PS129 A67 2019 | DDC 814/.0093564—dc23 LC
    record available at https://lccn.loc.gov/2019005313

Set in Filosofia by E. Cuddy.
Designed by N. Putens.

*To my parents, of course*

# CONTENTS

Spring, a few years ago: I dipped into a West Philadelphia coffee shop for something cold and caffeinated. I was on my way to teach, in the hometown I'd returned to after decades, and I needed a boost before facing three hours of manuscript scrutiny in an airless basement, the realm of adjuncts who have no pull. The café was less than a mile from the neighborhood where I had been born and raised: a progressive nest of professors and political activists and inter-*something* families, where sycamore roots erupted from brick sidewalks and Victorians that had been sectioned into apartments were being reconstituted as single-family homes.

I demolished half of my drink in one swallow and carried the remainder outside. A bright sun snapped me to attention; I tossed the cup into the nearest trash can. The urgency of that act—the automaticity of it—caught me up short, as did the sense of having done something wrong. *Look at that,* I said to myself, *I just broke a rule I didn't know I followed.* Having dispatched the iced coffee, I crossed the street, entered my building, and descended its wide marble staircase. Of course, I thought. My actions made perfect sense. Perfect sense for a black man in the 1930s, living in the Jim Crow South. None of which described me.

Summer, 1975 or 1976: I set out from my neighborhood to head for the one where I now teach. Back then, my interests were less academic. I cared about the campus shops that catered to students; the all-concrete swim club with a good cheesesteak place around the corner; boys from school I might run into if I took the right turns along the way. Did I have my teenage uniform on? The T-shirt and Army Navy Store overalls that I'd embroidered and patched to within an inch of their life? Was I wearing shoes? Probably, probably, maybe not.

I ambled along, carrying a can of soda—Frank's Black Cherry Wishniak or possibly a Dr. Pepper (both upstream flavors in a cola/uncola world). My father's car pulled up alongside me. He and my mother had split a few years prior; I saw him for weekly visits or when he drove by in his late-model Impala on the way to show a house or put up a For Sale sign. Dad's passenger-side window sank down (he had electric). He leaned over to speak. I doubt he bothered with hello.

*Should you be drinking like that on the street?*

My father didn't make us call him "sir" when we answered his questions, the way my uncles had raised my cousins to do. Nonetheless, my sisters and I had learned to answer without hesitation and never with slang or ambiguity. *Yes* or *no*, none of this *yeah* or *maybe* or *I don't know*. We learned not to hedge the start of a sentence with *I think . . .* because that prompted an immediate *You didn't think*.

But on that hot street and with my guard down, I did the unthinkable. I hesitated. I could not form a response because I did not understand his question. Sodas weren't forbidden. It was hot out. I'd certainly bought it with my own money. In that sliver of silence where I scrambled to make sense of his words, he dropped the matter. Another aberration.

"I'll see ya," he said, and drove off.

My father was born in 1926. He grew up in rural Georgia, where his own father wasn't known as the town's doctor or the town's colored doctor but the town's nigger doctor. Peonage farms and poll taxes were the order of the day, and black people landed on the chain gang for minor and manufactured infractions—claims of vagrancy, public drunkenness, loitering, or curfew violation. For residents of my father's neighborhood, Colored Folks Hill, every public action had consequence and every gesture was met with judgment. My grandfather never left the house without a necktie, even to go fishing and even in the bone-melting heat of the Jasper County summers. Why wouldn't my father flinch, some forty years later, when he saw me slurping down a soda on the sidewalk, an unguarded, unmasked teenager with not a care in the world? And I, his child—hardwired to win his affection and diffuse his ready anger—why wouldn't I absorb his admonishment, however irrelevant or confusing?

Most Americans know the adage, "The apple doesn't fall far from the tree." Germans have it too—"Der Apfel fällt nicht weit vom Stamm"— though they're specifically measuring the distance from fruit to trunk. The Spanish version has to do with splinters—"de tal palo tal astilla"— while the French rendition takes an absolutist tone, with "Les chiens ne font pas des chats."

In some way or another, most of us come to realize that we are, more or less and for better or worse, chips off the parental block. That fact alone is not what prompted me to commission the essays that fill this book. Instead, I was intrigued by what came *after* the sidewalk-borne shock of recognition: the curiosity and amusement and compassion and insight, palpable evidence that relationships continue to evolve as we make our way through life, even if one party (in my case, my father) is dead and gone. As the years go by, these discoveries pass through a different filter—one that's less reactive, more gentle. We begin to welcome these reflections and refractions, however they come. Unanticipated reckonings result, thanks to the discernment we've gained along the way, tempered as it is by firsthand exposure to birth and death, to faith and betrayal, to endurance and impermanence. What other inheritances, I wondered, could be explored through those flickers of likeness we stumble upon at events large and small: at weddings and wakes, at reunions and after goodbyes, from a gesture, a phrase, a glance?

I decided to ask people—interesting people, people who think deeply and write beautifully and come at life from multiple directions—to consider that space between the apple and the tree, to make meaning of it. And make meaning they do. Donna Masini and Angelique Stevens pay eloquent homage to the traits that have kept them anchored in a tempest-ridden world, while Kyoko Mori, Avi Steinberg, and John Freeman look at how they've redeployed problematic inheritances to more beneficial ends. (As John and I emailed back and forth about his essay, he made a point that struck me as representing the approach of every writer here. When one is writing about family, he noted, "love is in clarity, not sentiment.")

Lauren Grodstein and Karen Grigsby Bates write about the rituals of feeding, its pleasure and purpose. S. Bear Bergman credits all of his skills as a storyteller to his father, from speech patterns to hand gestures to how they take up space in a room. Several contributors, including Jane Hamilton, Leland Cheuk, and Marc Mewshaw, explore what it means to absorb only a fraction of the larger-than-life parent's personality; for Sallie Tisdale, Daniel Mendelsohn, and Clifford Thompson, enacting their mothers' behaviors serves to reframe history.

Ann Patchett and Laura van den Berg write about likenesses of the physical and paranormal variety. We hear from Shukree Hassan Tilghman on speaking the truth (except when it comes to superpowers) and Carolyn Ferrell on living the truth (no matter how hard it is to come by). Lizzie Skurnick considers the multigenerational love of language in her family, which is put to the test as one generation gains it and another loses it. Lolis Eric Elie also reflects through a multigenerational lens: As a first-time father, he wonders what legacies, beyond a name, he will pass on to his son and whether the good ones can be sifted out from the bad. Kate Carroll de Gutes and Mat Johnson reconsider their capabilities through the filter of a parent's dementia. And Susan Ito and Dana Prescott embrace the independent, adventure-driven spirits of their fathers, while Laura Miller unknowingly pays tribute by living the life her mother wanted but never had.

As a younger adult, any parental trait I came across was trotted off to the therapist's office to be dissected and then excised. Nothing was more important than being my own person (see soft drink choices above), and so any familial vestiges read as admonishments, warnings embedded in those tics, those mirrors, those patterns of speech. Four decades and a good amount of individuation later, when I tossed that drink into a curbside trash can and realized my father's social calculations had saturated my psyche, instead of being disturbed by the epiphany, I felt only comfort and curiosity. What other dictums and beliefs had been grafted onto me through example or instruction? And to what end? What purpose did any of them serve? With the perspective of age, I saw that one behavior, irrelevant as it was to my lived experience, forming a bridge between me and this person I had loved, despite his thick and brittle shell. In acting out my late father's practice, I felt his proximity. Other connections bloomed. What if, I wondered, and not without some astonishment, my stern and unyielding father allowed his street-side question to go unanswered because, in that confused silence, he grasped its irrelevance? Had my father actually backed down? I could recall no similar experience throughout my childhood, but one was enough to invert gravity.

Welcoming the likeness, the echo, isn't the same as according it value. My father delivered me into a world so different from his that such public cautions were unnecessary. I was acting out a race play that was asynchronous, out of step with my time. Still, it raised questions about whose life I was enacting, revelations about the disjunction between behavior and cultural context. What did this absorbed lesson contribute to the world, to me? If it wasn't needed for safety, maybe it offered a cautionary tale, a reminder of how insidious racism can be, a lesson that I would need less for my survival than for my humanity. To see past all the privileges accorded to me—to glimpse a world in which I would have had to relinquish that sidewalk, eyes lowered, whenever a white person approached—was, in fact, a gift.

On the following pages, this carefully curated band of writers, thinkers, and doers welcome their own trait-based epiphanies, seizing the chance to see themselves and their parents anew, and to share with readers the alchemy of how those components come together to produce a new sense of self, a new sense of their progenitors, and a new sense of belonging in the worlds that they and we inhabit.

The author, her father, and Storm, ca. 1968.

APPLE, TREE

# Predictions

LAURA VAN DEN BERG

My mother saw her first psychic when she was a young woman, nineteen or twenty, in her hometown of Nashville. Her father drove her over to a place in East Nashville, where she remembers a dramatic-looking woman (big earrings, a clamor of bracelets) swinging open the door. She can't remember why she sought the help of a psychic in the first place, only that this one had come recommended by her hairdresser, whom she trusted. If pressed, my mother imagines she was seeking help with boy trouble—*back then, that was always the story*. When I express surprise that my grandfather was a willing participant—he was a dairy farmer and not the type to put much stock in the otherworld-ly—my mother reminds me that he loved to drive. *He would take me on any kind of adventure if a car was involved.* My mother can't recall what she and her first psychic discussed, and while she never went back to this woman in East Nashville, nevertheless, the visit opened for my mother a portal into a world of mediums and predictors, a world that would captivate her for many years to come, a world she would pass on to me. When I ask my mother for a *why*, she tells me—*People have been trying to make sense out of chaos for millennia. That is what you hope a psychic can do.*

Writing a novel can feel like an attempt to make sense of chaos, so per-haps it's not a coincidence that I got my first tarot reading in Key West, during a summer spent at an artist's colony. I was struggling mightily

1

with my first novel, and at the height of my creative troubles, I found a man named Ron Augustine during the sunset celebration at Mallory Square, after I had read an article about him in *National Geographic*. Ron Augustine was easy to spot because he conducted his readings on the pier, holding a very large white parasol in one hand and turning the cards with the other. That summer marked six years of work on my first novel, and instead of the breakthrough I longed for, I kept hitting impasse after impasse. The book was under contract: I was starting to think I would never finish and would have to repay the advance. I told myself that I could live with either outcome; somehow I would figure out a way forward, even if I had to give the money back. I just wanted someone to tell me how it was all going to end. I could not stand the not knowing for a moment longer.

I waited in line to speak with Ron Augustine, and when it was my turn, I sat in a folding chair across from him. He laid the cards out on a small table and surveyed my fates. He told me that I had been engaged in a tough struggle for years and now that struggle was almost over. I was close, but I needed to keep pushing and I needed to be braver—braver than I had ever been before. I paid him, thanked him, and then cried while waiting in line for fried clams.

The next morning, I woke at dawn and set out for the ocean. From a dock, I dove into the water, and when I came up for air, the solution was right there, clear as a familiar song. I returned to my studio and deleted the last hundred pages of my novel, the section that had been giving me the most difficulty. I threw out my flash drives and emptied the trash on my laptop; I worked to eradicate any trace of those old pages. This was what I understood "brave" to mean: release what is not working and what will never work and make something new, something better, in that empty space. Deep down, I had wanted to make this move when I first arrived at the residency, but I was too scared. I rewrote those hundred pages in three weeks. I submitted the book to my editor on time; I did not have to repay the money after all. All the while, I wondered what would have happened had I not thought to seek out Ron Augustine, if a stranger with a parasol had not told me exactly what I needed to hear, at the exact right moment in time.

My mother believes mediums are better with the past than with the future. As an example, she cites a visit to Cassadaga, the famed medium community in Florida. In the seventies, my mother saw a psychic in Cassadaga who told her that her first cousin's wife had committed suicide—true—and that this dead woman now had a message for my mother. The problem is: Most people don't see psychics for information about the past. In Cassadaga, the information about the suicide was impressive, a testament to the medium's powers, but it was also information my mother already knew. Most people—certainly my mother, certainly me—are hungry for the predictive. For a glimpse into the future, which is in a sense a glimpse into the forbidden, for to know our own futures is a kind of power we are not supposed to have.

The best medium my mother says she ever saw was a man in California— except she never actually *saw* him. He was a telephone psychic, and for a period of five years, she spoke to him every four months. During this period, my parents were going through a painful, lengthy divorce, and my mother swears this man in California could predict what would happen in the courtroom, what my father's next move would be. My mother says that she hadn't wanted to hear things you could hear from your therapist or a friend—*hang in there, one day at a time*. She had wanted answers. She had wanted to *know*.

Alas, the story of the man in California does not have a happy ending. He was diagnosed with early onset dementia and lost his powers. My mother consulted a string of psychics afterward, hungry for the answers to keep coming, and felt that they all failed her.

A family story: My father was said to have ESP for a time, back when I was still a small child. Not psychic abilities per se, but a sixth sense, an ability to see several moves ahead—to predict how the weather would turn, what a person was going to do. Then one morning he was carrying an armful of dress shirts down the stairs. He stepped on a sleeve and somersaulted to the ground. The fall knocked him out, dislocated his shoulder, and after he came to in the ER, he never had ESP again.

The bottom line: Powers of all kinds are delicate. You never know what will make them leave.

In 2014 I was on the road a lot. At some point, I decided to embark on a little project where I would visit tarot card readers in each new destination. Probably I should have sought out a therapist instead, but I wanted my own answers and this project seemed like a shortcut to getting them.

At the time, I was bouncing around between various campuses, always between home and some other place. My husband and I were spending too much time apart. My father was ill. Out of nowhere, or so it seemed, I had been beset by crippling flying anxiety. I was in a state of perpetual motion, moving too fast to absorb much of anything.

Over the course of this experiment, I had tarot readings in Portland, Maine; New Orleans; LA; and Perth, Australia. The longest reading: sixty minutes. The shortest: ten. All the readers were women except for Ron Augustine in Key West. The readings cost somewhere between ten and sixty dollars, usually paid in cash. At the start of a reading, I always wanted to go straight to the bad stuff. That is the fiction writer in me, I think: Let's get right to the trouble.

In LA, the tarot reader told me a friend from childhood recently came back into my life and that this person did not wish me well. *Be careful*, she warned. I nodded because I did not know how to explain that I had very few friends in childhood and I was not in touch with any of them.

In Perth, the medium's address was a storefront for a crystals shop, the air inside clouded with dust and incense. When I told the owner I was looking for a reading, she bolted the front door and led me down a flight of narrow, winding steps, the ceiling treacherously low. I followed her into the basement and then another small room with a cement floor; she bolted this door behind us too. If she had been a man, I would have run screaming. We sat at a small table; she lit a cigarette. She chain-smoked through the entire reading and described the state of my life with alarming accuracy. At the end, she told me that I knew what I needed to do, and when I was ready, I would do those things.

During this experiment, I went to Chicago but did not get a reading. I only had so much time and decided to go to a museum instead.

Having felt misled by psychics during her divorce, my mother remains disillusioned with the whole enterprise. *I'm done with them*, she's told me time and time again, and yet I recently learned her disillusionment did not stop her from phoning a psychic recommended to her by a fitness instructor. This psychic was located in East Nashville too, not far from my mother's first encounter decades earlier, and she reports that absolutely none of his predictions have come to pass.

Aside from the man in California, my mother now thinks the most effective mediums she ever spoke to were not meant for people, but for animals. She reminds me of a family friend's story: They had a horse who started misbehaving, for reasons no trainer or vet could understand. Finally the family friend called a horse psychic, who reported that this horse was being driven mad by a ringing sound in her stall, like an alarm that wouldn't quit. *What ringing?* they thought at first, and then they remembered: The horse's stall had been changed, just before the bad behavior started, to next door to the barn office. The owners went and stood in the stall, and every time the office phone went off, a shrill ringing sounded out. Soon they could see why the phone had been driving the horse mad.

*I wonder if the difference is dealing in the now versus attempting to predict the future*, I say to my mother. People call animal communicators because their dog won't stop barking at the mailperson or because their cat seems depressed. The aim is diagnostic, not predictive, and perhaps the predictive is the problem with the whole medium enterprise, when it comes to people—or the problem with the particular feature of my inheritance. My mother and I want a key to the future. We want exactly what human consciousness is not designed to offer. If we know, we think we can prepare. A practical impulse, in some ways, if executed through a highly impractical means.

I don't feel disillusioned about mediums in the way my mother does, but in an effort to save money and to take fewer shortcuts, I haven't spoken to a psychic or tarot reader in a couple of years. My flying anxiety worsened, and then anxiety began to take root in other areas of my life, and my father got sicker—so I sought out a real therapist and began to do the hard work of dealing with the past and the now and the future.

One point of clarification—I haven't consulted a medium meant for *humans* in a couple of years. This spring, I consulted an animal communicator for my dog, in an effort to understand why my otherwise friendly running companion would bark at runners when he passed them on the trails. According to the animal communicator, my dog finds barking at runners "highly satisfying"—he knows I dislike this behavior and yet he has no plans to change. *Some things are too fun to give up*, he reportedly told the animal communicator. And when you put it that way, who could blame him? My dog also mentioned that he enjoys getting up on all the furniture except for a chair in the bedroom—the legs wobble and he slides around, once he even fell, a statement that startles me to my feet with its accuracy.

When I press my mother for specifics on the subject of psychics, she admits that she threw out all her notes from her readings during her last move. I never took notes during my own readings, even though I have a bad memory, another trait I share with my mother. But I keep circling back to the idea of the diagnostic versus the predictive, the now versus the future—and how maybe it's not so much that we want to know the future, for to truly *know* could be a grim and burdensome power, but rather we want confirmation for what we suspect might be true. Making big decisions can be so lonely, after all, and there is a special kind of power in a stranger telling you what you already know, in the deepest well of yourself. *Just keep going. You know what you need to do.* To hear a stranger, whether it be because they are a very canny reader of people or because they are in conversation with the divine, repeat back to you the truth that you have been hesitant to trust, the truth that you have tried to ignore or maybe even bury—but can't for a moment longer.

# Curtains

SALLIE TISDALE

I've lived in a garage, a dormitory, a screened-in porch, and more than one basement. I've owned three houses. After my divorce and the divestiture of common property, I moved into a small second-floor apartment in a large complex of handsome brick buildings originally used as military family housing. Here we have hardwood floors, tiny kitchens, big trees, lousy wiring.

Hardly anyone in the complex draws their curtains. I walk my dog in the evening, and behind the disguise of his slow rooting in the shrubbery, I get brief, cropped shots of other lives. A deer head with an impressive rack mounted on a wall painted navy blue. Two women at a dining table, heads close. A father drilling his kids in calisthenics, barking like a sergeant. A man practicing piano, the faint, rapid scales barely audible through the glass. A young couple, so unformed they seem to be made of putty, pushing a pair of Chihuahuas in a baby stroller down the walk. A dour woman sitting on the steps of the building where I get my mail, smoking. She refuses to move so I can enter; her profound distaste for the world seems immutable, genetic.

Below me, in #2, a couple approaches punk's middle age: she has ropy dreadlocks, and he has a ropy beard, and both have a lot of ink. Through the windows, I can see the Tibetan prayer flags, the bicycles, the aquarium. Sometimes I hear hammering below, and their bulldog yaps every time I pass the door. In six years as neighbors, we have learned each other's names and exchange occasional comments about the weather. Once I helped them jump their car battery, but I have never been in their apartment. When our basement storage units are broken into, I wake them up early in the morning with the news. It is a voyeur's dream come true, the storage units open, spilling out contents: A dishwasher. Bicycles. An artificial Christmas tree. Dog crate. Old skis. An antique mirror. We pad around the mess in our pajamas, in our sudden, brief intimacy, sorting out what is theirs and what is mine. And what is mine to know.

My parents live in the same house for thirty years. It is built for them by his father, next door to the house where my father grew up. Eventually they buy that house too, and then two more on the block. She teaches at the elementary school we attend, and my father teaches at the high school. My mother knows more about everyone in the neighborhood than she would like to know. And everyone in town knows who we are, knows our lives. Thinks they know.

I babysit for the couple next door until my grandfather dies and the family is evicted so my grandmother can move in. She spends every afternoon in our living room. Her sisters live up the hill with my ancient cousins, and my mother hosts every family dinner; our relatives fill two tables and use every dish in the house. Twice a year, we drive several hours south to visit my mother's family. She sits with her mother and her sister at the dining table; they bend their heads together, relaxed and girlish, laughing for hours. My mother, giggling. Then we drive back.

My life is irregular, with an abundance of solitude. I work odd hours. I leave for a few days, or a few weeks. I sometimes wonder what the neighbors in #2 make of me, what the young couple with the baby stroller or the man shouting cadence to his sons assume about me, the woman in #4: older, alone, lives with a dog, ducks out in her pajamas every morning for the newspaper. I doubt they notice the lopsided, oblique state of my life. And I always close the curtains at night. There's a good chance they don't notice me at all. Their passing glances are nothing more than that, which is all I give to them.

My peeking in, this urge to see what's hidden through knotholes and between unused curtains—like a lot of things we prefer to think are obscure, this one's fairly obvious. All those crowded family dinners. Decades later, I keep a lot of secrets and try to ferret out everyone else's. I strive not to be entirely known, even when I am aching for it. Sister, cousin, neighbor: our lives are filled with people to whom we are nothing else. To whom we are set in stone and time from the moment we meet. And I don't really want to know their lives; I want to imagine them, to pretend I know, to fill in gaps and guess at meaning. To write their stories, however wrong the details.

Her life: She is never alone. She is up at six in the morning. Every morning. She lets the dog out into the yard, wakes three children, makes them breakfast, then carries a Bloody Mary into the master bedroom for my father, who has a hangover. She goes to work. She comes home from work. She parks her car in the garage every day. She makes dinner every evening and washes the dishes after and then drops into her chair. My father is asleep in a beer cloud on the couch, and the three children are lined up in front of the television. She lights a cigarette, sighs, and picks up her book.

She shops at Safeway every Saturday and puts away the groceries and then prepares lessons for the coming week. She gets her hair done every Thursday after work, lying back under the bulbous hairdryer for an hour, the machine's roar her only silence. She pays the bills on Sunday afternoons, papers strewn across the white table, chewing Ayds candies because she is always dieting. The evening roast thaws on the counter.

In the summer, we go to the mountain cabin for two weeks. She makes dinner every evening on a wood stove in the light of a kerosene lantern and washes the dishes after with water drawn by the bucket from a spring. My father is drinking beer on the deck, and the three children are up in the sleeping porch, reading comics by flashlight. She drops into her lawn chair on the deck and picks up her book with a sigh.

When my son is sixteen, a miserable, handsome mess of a boy, he is desperate to own a black leather jacket. He is sure the jacket is all he needs;

it will complete the Doc Martens and the shoe-black pompadour; it will complete the cool that seems to elude him. I try to explain that coolness is internal, born of confidence, that he is already cool. He doesn't seem to hear a word I say.

I see my children. But they don't see me. They don't really think about me, at all—not about me, the person, the intricate bundle of needs, desires, and gifts wound together into a self unlike any other. They don't think about my life, my successes, my worries. Children aren't supposed to see their parents. If all goes well, a parent's life is under wraps, and all the child sees is what they can depend upon; they see safety and pay it no mind.

My father goes into the navy out of high school and is sent into the Pacific theater for the last harrowing year of war. He comes home, enrolls in the local college, flunks out the first semester, and transfers to the state school, where he meets my mother. Where his attention knocks her over like a sledgehammer.

In an old photograph, she wears a tense smile, her feet neatly tucked beneath the circle skirt. She is sitting on the lawn near a group of handsome, laughing men and women. My father is in the middle of the group. She is there because he invited her, because she would never go where she was not invited. She is cheerful because being cheerful is part of being a good girl. She does not allow the stomach-cramping anxiety to show. She is clean and well-groomed and appropriate and almost invisible in this lush garden of blond hair and young muscle. My father is relaxed, charming—quick with a joke, a great whistler, smart and good with his hands. He slicks back his dark hair and mugs for the camera.

She finishes school, the first person in her family to graduate from college, and begins to teach. Her sister and cousins and friends are already having babies, but she wants to teach, she holds out. He finishes a year later, and they are married the year after that. They move to the small town where he was born, where I will be born, where they will settle into place like a fallen anchor. Where he will trade most of the rakish grins for a frown, the lean silhouette for a big belly hard as lead. Where he will hold a newborn in one hand and a beer in the other, gazing at the camera with a puzzled look. One, two, three babies in four years, and then a fourth one who never takes a breath, and a trip to the doctor so it can't happen again. She will teach, she will go back to work. She will not stay home with children any longer than this.

I make dinner almost every evening, wash dishes afterward, fall with a sigh onto the couch, and reach for a book. Or the *New York Times* or a magazine or the remote. Or the car keys. I head out into the rain with quick steps, sketching a wave at the couple with the new pit bull. I know they know nothing about me.

When I am fourteen, my father is hospitalized with what seems to be appendicitis and then abruptly put in intensive care with pancreatitis, an alcoholic's disaster long in the making. He lies unconscious for days in the whirring hush. In the middle of the timeless, uncertain hours, my mother sits at the white Formica table with its neat piles of bills and taxes, the filing and homework, and tells me that she'd made my father get more life insurance the year before. She talks quietly, steadily, without tears. I am so struck that she is talking to me like this at all, talking to me for the first time in my life as though I am an adult, telling me a secret for the first time, that I barely register what she says. That she expected this. That all the compromise, the accommodation, the hiccups from postwar youth to everything else, led to this, and she saw it coming. Her fortuitous planning is an irony we never discuss again; she dies of cancer long before he does.

This is me peeking in her window between the half-drawn curtains and telling her story. Which is part of my story.

I stand outside, looking through her half-drawn curtains, trying to read her story. Which is part of my story. I wonder if I am like my mother. But I don't know. What was my mother like?

# Lies My Parents (Never but Maybe Should've) Told Me

SHUKREE HASSAN TILGHMAN

It was snowing that Christmas Eve in 1984. Or maybe there was just snow on the ground. Snow was on the rooftop for sure. I remember that. I saw it as I approached my aunt's white split-level house. The paint was peeling a bit near the windows. The yard was plain with a sad tree and a chain-link fence. The driveway wasn't paved, just scattered with tiny gravel. This side of town was a place where working poor people lived and scraped to keep the lights on, but it was an otherwise nice house in Blacktown. As a little kid, I didn't know "Blacktown" was a euphemism for "where black people live" and not the actual name of the section of small-town Bridgeville, Delaware, which my mother and I now called home.

I spotted the snowy roof as I came in from the car with my cousin Hakim, ten months my senior, my aunt Veronica, and my mother, Eleanor. I still found it strange arriving at this house, like I was coming to visit a family member and then suddenly realizing that family member is me. I'd only been living there a few weeks. My mother and father had some disagreement that I was too young to know about and we'd moved in with my aunt. My cousin Hakim and I were like brothers. The first grandchildren in a big family that all lived in the same small town, we saw each other virtually every day. Living together seemed natural to me, even exciting.

I don't remember missing my dad. Probably because he lived down the street. In that house, the one we'd left—and where we'd return a few months later—there was no talk of this mythic top-of-house-bound figure called Santa Claus and how he was going to bring presents for me and all the other kids in the world on Christmas Eve, when he parked his sleigh and reindeers on the roof. This fascinating new concept had just been brought to my attention by Hakim, who, in his ten months' worth of days longer on the earth, had become knowledgeable about a generous and magical white man in a velvet red suit with furry white trim whose friends called him Kris. That's why I was standing outside studying the roof of my new home. I was obsessed. I was five. Santa is the first lie I remember being told. And thanks to my parents, that beautiful, innocent fantasy would soon crumble under the crushing weight of the truth.

A little over a year ago, my wife and I welcomed our first child, a baby girl. Decisions about what kind of parents we would become began immediately. There were, of course, the practical: What to name the baby. Breastfeed or bottle-feed? Did we have the right car seat? There were also the seemingly frivolous: What clothes would we dress her in to leave the hospital? The hand-me-downs from friends and family or the cheap big-box-chain-store clothes that come ten to a hanger in various colors or a special outfit with a name you would know on the label—which would best suit this wardrobe change from the first act in the womb to the rousing second act that is early life? Did we even remember to bring clothes? (For the record, we went chain store, after almost forgetting to bring anything at all.)

The decisions never end. And however large or small those decisions appear at the time, the results of each one forms small elements of our child's character, of her view of the world and her place in it, of who she will become. If our daughter comes home from the hospital in a designer baby outfit, for example, and that becomes part of the narrative she comes to know about herself, the pictures she sees of it, then *we've* formed part of that identity for her. She's someone who wears Ralph Lauren at one day old, whatever that might mean—vanity, bourgeois waste, or simply appreciation of a good stitch.

For better or worse, our parents or guardians tell us who we are through their actions, deeds, and words. We depend on them to do that until we are adult enough to determine who we are for ourselves. Even then, our brains are wired with the messages long after our conscious minds have forgotten. Thus is the power of parenting. But what to make of the lies they tell us? What value does the truth hold? When do I lie to my daughter, and when do I tell her the truth?

The snow was piled three or four inches high on the slanted roof of the Blacktown house as we approached. I wondered out loud, "How is Santa Claus going to land on that snowy roof, park all his reindeer, sling a huge bag of presents over his shoulder, and not slip and fall off the roof or all the way down the chimney?" I was plagued by the image of big jolly Santa with his big jolly belly and his big jolly cheeks and his big jolly bag of presents, screaming a big jolly, "Oh shhhhit!" as his boots shot upward, he tumbled awkwardly onto his shoulder and careened off the roof, hitting the ground with a thud just in front of the front porch, right about where we were standing. He'd be hurt, I thought, but there was reason to believe he'd end up fine on account of his belly being like a giant dodge ball that would bounce him off the ground a few times before finally coming to rest. But he definitely wouldn't want to deliver any toys to kids in the house with the slippery roof on which he just busted his ass. This was my fear.

That night, Hakim and I tried our best to stay awake. Our plan was to wait until Santa showed up; then, when we heard him coming down the chimney, pretend to be asleep. Everyone knows you can't be awake when Santa's in the house or else he won't leave anything—another piece of Christmas knowledge to which I was recently hipped. Just as we drifted off, I heard something: a rumbling followed by the thud of footsteps, then a man's voice. Hakim looked at me with giant eyes as if, despite his confident swagger in espousing the characteristics of St. Nick, he couldn't believe what he was hearing.

"Santa?" he asked. Then, in the affirmative. "It's Santa. Told you!"

I was speechless. "We have to go to sleep!" Hakim yelled in a whisper. He slammed his eyes shut before I could respond. I quickly closed my eyes too, adding a gaping mouth to sell it, and in a moment, I was asleep.

When I woke up that Christmas morning, I was so bleary, and the dawn so early, that I almost didn't remember it being Christmas. Suddenly the wave of memory washed over me. I woke up Hakim, we raced downstairs, and I began tearing open my presents. My mother came out of the kitchen drinking coffee with my father. For some reason, I didn't bother to question how or when he'd arrived. I don't remember what the presents were, but they were all magical. The whole experience was. It wasn't my first Christmas, but it was the first one I remember, the first one I was conscious. I loved it.

I must've praised the name of the man from the North Pole a little too much during my revelry because later in the day, when things had calmed down, my mother and father pulled me into a private conversation. They sat me down. There was a long pause. Then my father gave my mother a look like, "You handle this one." She got right to the point:

"There's no Santa Claus, honey. No rosy-cheeked white man in a suit comes around to give you presents. I give you presents. Me. And your father. And we work hard all year long to give you these presents because we love you. Not no white man in a suit. That's just pretend. You understand?"

But those sounds? The thud of footsteps, the man's voice?

It suddenly hit me that it was my mother opening the door for my father, who was bringing over presents, and his boots stomping the floor as he knocked snow off them and onto the mat. In retrospect, what I heard, the reality, was as magical as the fantasy. It was two people who weren't getting along, at an impasse in their marriage, working together to provide something special for their child. It was love. It was parenting. And it was real.

After some silent processing, my excitement running cold in the light of truth, I turned my head up to my parents.

"Yes," I said, trying to mask the crushing of my world.

My mother softened, rubbed my head.

"It's okay to play pretend. I just don't want to you to be confused. You need to know who does things for you and who doesn't. Why should Santa Claus get the credit?"

At the time I must've been confused as to what that meant. I can't imagine I had any notion of "credit"—who deserves it and who doesn't. But this was a mantra repeated over and over throughout the years, well past the time that I would have ever still believed in Mr. Claus. It's the one that sticks with me: "Why should Santa Claus get the credit?" For most of my adult life I was torn about that sentiment. Frankly, it seemed petty, my parents in a struggle for credit with a fictional character. Now that I'm a parent, I say, why should he? Parenting is HARD. Scratching up money to pay bills and provide presents around Christmas time is HARD. To Hell with Ol' Saint Nick.

I have already lied to my child. I didn't realize it until recently. My daughter's starting to stand up on her own. With increasing regularity, she pulls herself up to a standing position and hangs out there trying to decide whether she'll walk. Instinctively she seems to know that taking a step is a decision between forward movement and falling. But she doesn't yet seem to know that the falling involves pain. Mostly because every time she starts to lose her balance or when it appears that she might fall, my wife or I catch her. Not every single time. We've let her fall back on her butt, or on a knee. But if it looks like a big tumble is imminent or a fall will be onto something that might actually hurt, we step in.

We're lying to her. *I'm* lying to her. Not even a good, conscious, full-throated lie about morality or the creation of the universe, but an inadvertent mistake of a lie about something as simple as walking.

I'm telling her she can learn to walk without experiencing pain. That mommy or daddy will be there to protect her from the big falls. But that's not possible. Not in walking across the living room, nor in her walk through life. Soon, any day now, I'm going to tell her the truth. I'm going to let her fall. Even when I know it's going to hurt. I can't help it. It's a behavior I inherited from the people who raised me, and I'm reminded every time I look down at my stomach.

In the same white house where I waited for Santa, I used to watch my mother iron my clothes. What seemed like every morning, she'd lay out my wares for the day and strike up the iron. Steam would shoot out of it and into the sky with a whistle. She'd lay the metal part of the iron on the clothes, move it back and forth, and magically the creases and wrinkles would disappear. I thought it was amazing. I begged my mother every morning for the opportunity, the privilege, the honor of helping her iron. She obliged, letting me place my hand on hers while she moved across the garments, eliminating the imperfections. Eventually, helping her didn't satisfy my need for independence. So I asked to do it myself.

She said no. I whined.

The next morning I asked again. She said no. This time I managed to push out some tears during my whine.

I pushed out tears the next few times I asked. Over and over. For days on end. Each time a no. Then, I became strategic. I didn't ask every day. I spaced out the asks. Still, no. One morning my mother laid out my clothes on the bed in the room where I was playing, shirtless. She plugged in the iron and left the room. As the steam rose and the seconds my mother was out of the room grew longer, my curiosity increased until it was unbearable. I moved the clothes and the towel they were on down to the floor. I arranged them, straightened out the shirt. I carefully grabbed the hot iron by the handle and tentatively put it down onto the shirt. The iron sizzled and hissed. I started moving it back and forth like I had seen hundreds of times. The bliss of independence and older-ness rushed through my body like a drug. The iron wasn't a toy. This wasn't pretend. I was actually ironing like a real person. And hell, it was *easy*. For those moments, I was never more aware of what it meant to feel pride.

"Hey! What are you doing?" my mother said sharply as she came upon the sight. She motioned for the iron. "Give that to me."

"Nooooooo!!" I screamed back, stopping her in her tracks. "I can do it!" I said with indignation as tears of frustration welled. "I can do it!"

My mother stepped back and, as calm as ever, replied,

"No, you can't. But fine, go ahead. Try."

With that, she left the room (though she later told me she was actually standing just outside the door, peeking in). Alone, and free at last, I resumed my task.

It was going great, moving the iron back and forth, until it was time to flip over the shirt. I tried to turn the iron back upright so I could do just that, but the iron was heavy and unruly. As I struggled to balance it in my little hand, the hot metal side jerked toward me. Instead of dropping the iron, I instinctively pressed it against my stomach to hold it up.

The burn was instant. It peeled my skin along a straight line that outlined the iron's metal edge. I screamed. And screamed.

My mother was furious when she came back in the room. The kind of angry that seemed directed more at herself than the wailing little boy in front of her. I don't think she knew I would burn myself. Maybe she thought I would just burn a finger, cry, and then forget the whole endeavor. Burning half my stomach wasn't in her imagined results. But she let me fall. She didn't lie to me. As a result, I got an important lesson in courage, boundaries, and the balance between the two.

This went on throughout childhood and adolescence. My parents would dole out the cold hard truth like it was medicine for the illusion inclined. I asked why it was chilly in the house—again. The furnace is broken, and there's no money to fix it. Why? Because they don't pay teachers in this country and we're broke.

I got suspended from school in the second grade, and my usually discipline-oriented parents let me off the hook after they met with the teacher. Why? Because that white lady is a racist. She's not like the white people on our street or your friends' parents. She doesn't like black kids. You remember that.

Politicians lie. Jesus isn't going to save you. They won't let a black man be president. Don't believe everything you read. Cartoons peddle stereotypes. Dogs bite. The good guys don't always win. Elvis is not the King of rock 'n' roll. Pro-life means men trying to tell women what to do with their bodies. There's a hole in the ozone, and yes, it might kill us all. I believe I was eight for those last two.

I'm still not sure how much of this was useful, accurate, or necessary for me to know. It was a stream of information that complicated the world and made gray the areas most kids see as black and white. Probably for good reason.

When I was growing up, I watched my two uncles morph from funny, energetic, well-kept young men to less funny, sometimes frantic, some-times haggard guys who sweat a lot and didn't ever seem to wear clean clothes. "They're drug addicts," one of my parents explained when I asked about the transformation. "Crack cocaine. It messes with your mind. See what it's done to them? Don't ever do that." That's the problem with the truth. Heroes die easy in the light of it.

Maybe that kind of reality check is inevitable. Perhaps, viewing the world around us with less of a naive lens is just the story of living. Eventually the world will become gray, the sooner we know that the better. How can I still let my kid be a kid?

When last Christmas rolled around and our daughter, seven months old, was about to experience it for the first time, my wife and I faced another early decision in the long line of decisions of what lies or truths to tell our daughter. No, she couldn't understand one way or the other whether Santa was real. But family members wanted that picture on Santa's lap you get from the local mall. I had to get creative in the truth-telling department, lest I start down a Santa road from which I can't turn back. Solution: Black Santa Claus. We found the mall with the black Santa Claus and got the pictures. Later, we'll tell her Santa isn't real. When she looks at that picture of herself in the lap of the smiling black Santa Claus, she'll know that the man depicted in the picture is a fantasy character. But at least he'll bear some resemblance to me, to one of the people who truly makes Christmas presents happen. And if I can get away with it, I'll tell her it's me in costume.

Perhaps my folks didn't lie to me enough, or perhaps they knew enough to know that the world is already chockfull of lies and illusions that would be impossible to avoid. As my parents, they could try their best to control the story they *could* control. And so they were honest. Honest to the point of destroying comfortable fantasies, be they about Santa Claus or the perfection of adults. Or revealing shortcomings that may burn us now but save us from greater harm in the future.

There was a lot of truth, but there were also lies. I used to believe that I was a He-Man-like character who got his power from the sun. I would stand out on our porch and stare at the sun with my arms flexed like a body builder. Other kids would make fun of me: "You're going to blind yourself, Shu!" Yet when I asked about this ability, my parents both said, "Yes, Shukree, of course you can get your power from the sun. Just don't look directly at it."

Those are the kind of lies I intend to tell my daughter. The ones that imbue you with power you may not otherwise believe you have. Those are the lies that are worth it.

My daughter can't form words yet. But soon enough, she's going to ask me things. About me, about my wife, about our house, our marriage, about our world, about how things work, where the boundaries are, why certain things don't make sense, about what it means to be black in the United States. Lying to her is inevitable. Sometimes lying is loving. But I'm going to do my best to tell the truth when it's appropriate, even when it's scary for me to do so. Just this afternoon, she stood up, balancing herself on the couch, and reached one leg forward while taking one hand off the couch and raising it in the air. Shakily, she looked at me, as if seeking permission. I know if she lifts the other hand, she will fall. But I look back at her and nod:

"You can do it, honey."

# Better Angels

CLIFFORD THOMPSON

I.

In the little house in northeast Washington DC where I grew up, I had
wonderful Christmases with my family, in spite of what occurred every
Christmas Eve, as dependably as the playing of the Nat King Cole album,
as the hanging of our plastic mistletoe, as the arrival of the holiday itself:
my mother's foul mood.

Those moods were different from her foul moods of the rest of the year,
which were infrequent but, maybe for that reason, memorable. On those
unpredictable occasions, you would come home, and though nothing in
particular seemed to have happened, though nothing in particular, in
fact, *had* happened, your normally easygoing, not-very-large mother
was suddenly five feet three inches of indignation, yelling at you about
the horrifying state of the house. It didn't matter that you spent an hour
several nights a week dreamily handwashing the dishes (as I did), or that
a week earlier you had vacuumed the house from top to bottom—the stove
was grimy, you could write your name in the dust on the furniture, and
let's not even talk about your bedroom. There was no arguing with her,
"argue" implying that the other person is listening. Once, while she was
taking a breath, I said something like, "Ma, I try, but sometimes I have
homework I have to . . . ," to which she replied, "And the kitchen floor
needs washing!"

I won't go into who was right. For one thing, I am no more objective
on this score than I was in the 1970s, when all of this was happening; for
another, Ma isn't around to defend herself; and last, what I find more

interesting than whether or not her tirades were justified is why and how they came about. As already noted, nothing in particular appeared to set them off; they seemed to result, rather, from the slow accumulation of smothered annoyance that one day (an excellent day to spend at a friend's house) could be smothered no more.

My point is that Ma's Christmas Eve foul moods were different. She didn't yell. She didn't *talk*. She would retreat to her bedroom, off the top of the stairs, and if my older siblings, my grandmother, or I tried to talk to her when she was on her way there, her response, if there was one, tended not to encourage further conversation. That suggests to me that she wasn't angry at *us*, exactly—otherwise, as with her bad moods at other times of the year, she would have told us why, and in great detail. Possibly she herself didn't know quite who or what she was angry at, or else she lacked the words to say. I don't remember those Christmas Eve moods occurring before my father's sudden death, in November 1974, which may provide a clue. Ma was only fifty when he died, and the years they had together were cut short; meanwhile, her years of taking care of her mother, which had begun when Ma was a young married woman, seemed to be without end. Perhaps Ma felt she'd been dealt a bad hand, and she was angry at the Dealer. Perhaps, at the time of the year for celebrating that particular entity, when she was supposed to feel happy and grateful, something in her said *No*.

These are guesses, substitutes for the definitive answers I'll never have. But here are some things about my mother that no one who knew her would dispute: She was a kind, warm, down-to-earth person. She would laugh at any joke or anecdote I told her, often starting to chuckle before I was finished, appreciating the fact of the funny story as much as the story itself; when one of my sisters had to leave in the dark to teach in the mornings, my mother would walk with her to the bus stop to make sure she was safe—never mind that she then had to walk back home by herself. To this day, my older cousins tell me stories about Ma from when they used to visit our house. How she'd slip my sweet-toothed cousin an extra piece of chocolate cake, let his sister (her namesake) get away with more backtalk than they both knew she should, and keep an eye on when competitive kids' games threatened to get out of hand.

Ma was generous in ways big and small. On her postal clerk's salary, she paid for my education at a pretty expensive college, even after I (a) nearly flunked out my freshman year and then (b) had the nerve to apply thousands of her hard-earned dollars toward a degree in creative writing. One day during my freshman year, I somehow thought it would be a good idea to make a surprise visit home—with three other people. When two young white women (one of them my girlfriend), a young Chinese-American man, and I—I being the only one my mother knew from Adam's housecat—showed up at her tiny house in her entirely black neighborhood, where many would have treated this little trio like space aliens, what did Ma do? Exactly what I knew she would: she sat with us in the little living room—the floor now crowded with my and my friends' backpacks and other crap—and asked who was hungry, who needed a drink, who needed the bathroom.

Ma's easygoing nature, I think now, led paradoxically to behavior that one would have described as anything but easygoing. Because she was usually so kind, she didn't bark every day I failed to dust (which was pretty much every day) or every time the Dirt Army recaptured ground in the Battle of the Bathroom; she kept her frustration to herself, until, as we have seen, it erupted. She raged, I think, at the unfairness of it, an idea that extended to other areas too. Virtue was not its own reward—some part of her believed she was owed something for her kindness, and when she felt she wasn't getting it, the result was sometimes not pretty.

That brings me to the Awards Night Episode. For three years beginning when I was eleven—the year my father died—I belonged to the Boy Scouts of America's Troop 77, which met weekly in the basement of a local church. Once a year came awards night, and one year our scoutmaster, Mr. Moses, a no-nonsense but good-natured Vietnam veteran in his late twenties, decided to recognize a few of the parents (mostly mothers in our largely fatherless group) who had helped him. The honorees did not include my mother, for the simple and very good reason that she was not involved at all with the troop. One day I walked into our dining room, the center of family activity, to find Ma sitting at the table, looking disgusted. "I hate to say this about your Mr. Moses, but I can't stand him," she told me, going on to report that she had telephoned Mr. Moses to ask why others had been honored but not her. (Why I wasn't too mortified to attend meetings after that, I don't know.)

Ma sorted mail on the night shift. That meant that she slept during the day, which, as she must have told me two hundred times, was "not like sleeping at night." Until you had done that, you hadn't worked. Apparently I wasn't working during the summer of 1982, when I was nineteen and between my freshman and sophomore years of college. Living at Ma's house, I had a job in northwest DC, delivering packages on foot with a handcart for an office-supply store. At the end of every day, I got paid $27.25 in cash. I was not exactly Agent 007 in Her Majesty's Secret Service, but I loved it. I got to be outside most of the time; every day I socked away $10 of my earnings, and I spent the rest hanging out with friends—drinking beer, going to movies, wasting time in video arcades, trying ineptly to meet young women, and generally having a good time. Still, because I was brought up with the unspoken but prevalent idea that if you were truly enjoying yourself, you were probably forgetting something crucial, I wasn't really surprised one day when, as I was passing my mother's bedroom, where she sat on the edge of the bed, she called me in.

"What's up?" I said, sitting beside her.

"I'm just waiting for you to slow down," she said. "You know, there's more to life than movies and video games. And before you tell me you're working, keep in mind I've got the hardest shift of all." The other things in life, she went on to explain, included cleaning the house. I reminded her that I had done chores, including washing dishes (a nightly event) and recently vacuuming the whole place, from the top floor to the basement— admittedly the two activities I tended to fall back on in these exchanges. She said about my vacuuming the house, "Well, it needs it again."

The house may have needed cleaning. She might simply have told me that, except that her real message was something else—expressed in the words "There's more to life than movies and video games," which, if you rearrange the letters, spells out, "Who are you to enjoy life when I don't?"

Some ideas—*I will never be like my parents*, for example—seem to be self-evident truths, to be superfluous predictions of the inevitable, rather than promises that should be made. For that reason, we often don't bother making them. But, oh, maybe we should.

## II.

Not long ago, my wife told me what a kind and generous person I am. "The problem," she added, "is that you know it."

That is to say: The wrongness of any insult or act of unfairness against me is compounded by the fact that someone is wronging, well, *me*, in all my obvious goodness.

If that's not bad enough, I deal with insults in an unfortunate way. It's as if the part of my brain that processes them is a bureaucracy, so bloated and inefficient as to be nonfunctional. First, a whole department has to conclude that, yes, there appears to be a breach in the system's normal good cheer, that—though one hesitates to jump to conclusions—something has been said that appears to have caused a slight darkening of overall mood. That cautiously reached judgment is communicated via interdepartmental channels to a separate unit, which makes the official determination that the system has indeed received what might be interpreted as an insult. By that time, of course, the insulter and I have said goodbye for the evening, he or she in good cheer, I wearing a smile that, if you look closely, has something odd going on around the eyes. Meanwhile, the bureaucratic wheels have continued to turn at their barely visible pace, until the Determination of Insult form has been officially submitted to the Department of Stewing.

This is an inheritance from my mother. I didn't realize the extent of the inheritance, though, until one day in June 1993, when I was thirty years old. I was with my wife, who was pregnant with our first child, on a car trip through Arizona and Colorado. (My wife and I together make up one driver. I have the license—which I received at sixteen, on my third try, from a woman who had an air of acting against her better judgment—and my wife has the sense of direction and decision-making ability. That is why we live in New York, with its extensive, all-night subway system.) At one point in our car trip, when we had been driving for hours and the sun was sinking toward the horizon, we were having terrible trouble finding something my wife insisted that we find (I've long since forgotten what). Finally we decided to give up and just stop and eat. When we got out of the car, my wife started to laugh, gently, at our fruitless efforts; she was not laughing at me but attempting to laugh with me, in a spirit of commiseration, as if the day's misadventure had been as much my idea as hers—and that, for some reason, was when I lost it. This was not the mere testiness of someone who had gotten lost while driving; this was the accumulated rage from every instance of unfairness, from every slight, real or perceived, from my wife or from others, that I had swallowed in recent memory, a rage beneath whose floorboards was the belief that I was a good guy who deserved better. As I presented my wife with a list of her supposed faults and offenses, I didn't recognize the growls coming from my throat as my own voice. Eventually I calmed down, my skin went from Hulk green back to its usual medium brown, and we walked quietly into the restaurant. We were eating when, suddenly, my wife put her hand over her mouth and crumpled into tears. I apologized, helplessly, feeling as bad as I ever have in my life. And here is where that promise to myself—the one I never made—might have helped.

I will never be the kind of person who responds to every annoyance, every verbal jab, wittily and in the moment, allowing me to forget it all afterward; I have, though, tried to be better at acknowledging anger before it builds in me. Still, to a large extent, we simply are who we are, and in some ways the past three decades have been one long lesson in the various ways that I am like my mother. Make yourself comfortable while I explain.

At eighteen I decided I was a writer. In college I had a writing pro-fessor, a short-story specialist of some renown, who one day told me two things I've never forgotten. She said, first, that I was her favorite writer in our class, which made me happy, of course, but also struck me even then as something a teacher should never say; indeed, I have taught writing myself now for several years, and I would never say that to a student, whether I thought it or not. My professor wanted me to know, second, that my work would probably not have "ferocious commercial appeal"—her exact words—which has turned out to be inaccurate only in that it was an understatement. I never stopped writing; for many years I published a short story or (much more often) an essay here and there, but for the longest time I was unable to sell a book. In my forties I wrote a novel that I believed in enough to self-publish after I had failed to find a traditional publisher. When I finally published a book—a collection of essays—the old-fashioned way, I had a party that doubled as my fiftieth-birthday celebration.

I supported myself all that time by editing. I worked at one company for nearly two decades and then, when that place folded, got a job as publications editor at a nonprofit, where I was never very happy and which I left after a couple of years. I was there one afternoon when my phone rang and, fully expecting the caller to be our in-house designer—a woman I always described as Edith Bunker without the sweetness—I sighed and answered it. The caller, instead, was a woman who informed me that the foundation she represented was so enamored of my writing that they were giving me $50,000. A month later I stood on a stage while arguably the nation's best-known playwright, a past recipient of the award, read aloud from the foundation's glowing description of my work.

These are, of course, the kinds of moments every writer dreams of, and make no mistake, they are moments I will take to my grave. You might think that one who has had this kind of luck, in a field that *no one forced him to enter*, would forever lose any right to complain; and in fact, my wife, who has listened to me gripe over the years about the state of my career, said something very much to that effect. But to think this way is to underestimate the human tendency toward dissatisfaction. My own dissatisfaction—which is the definition of what are called first world problems—stems from the fact that, award or no award, my work remains obscure. And this is where Ma comes in. When I hear other writers interviewed on National Public Radio, when I see profiles of them in the *New York Times*, part of me thinks: *Who are you to enjoy such prominence when I don't?* Promises, promises . . .

What do we do with these parts of ourselves? Maybe, as with anger, they need to be acknowledged and thereby controlled; maybe, then, we can encourage those better angels of our nature. For me, those, like the other parts, come largely from my mother. Any generosity in me, I owe to her; I told her so the day before she died. And if I love to laugh, it's because she did too.

In their later years, my mother and grandmother lived with one of my sisters, but a big part of caring for Grandma—who lived to 106 years old—fell to Ma in her retirement. My mother had some bitter moments over this. "It's like a joke," she said to me one day in exasperation. "An old lady taking care of an older lady." My mother, unlike her youngest child, actually had something to complain about. But she could laugh about it too. And I laugh sometimes, even now, when I think of a story she told me over the phone one day. Ma, who was about seventy at the time, was at home with my grandmother, who was about a hundred. My grandmother, a worrier from way back, had reached the point where she couldn't watch anybody leave the room without fearing that she'd never see the person again. "I went to the basement," Ma told me, "and I could hear her talking to herself the whole time. When I came back upstairs, she said, 'Thank you, Jesus!'" At that point in the story I laughed so hard I fell over sideways on the sofa, and on the other end of the phone, Ma was laughing with me.

# The Only Light We've Got

ANGELIQUE STEVENS

For, while the tale of how we suffer, and how we are delighted, and
how we may triumph is never new, it always must be heard. There isn't
any other tale to tell, it's the only light we've got in all this darkness.
—JAMES BALDWIN, "Sonny's Blues"

It was a running joke between my sister, stepdad, and me. "When we can't
afford to eat, we'll just sell some of your mother's books." My stepdad's
Boston accent still thick after fifty years in Rochester made it sound like
"yuh muthah." He had been married to Mom since we were babies, so we
called him Dad. When it was time to move yet again, the four of us would
pack all of our belongings, including the furniture, into one truckload
before off-loading into an apartment not much bigger than the truck.
We moved almost a hundred times by the time I was out of the house.
Sometimes Dad would go on another bender and lose his job, or Mom
would go back into the psych ward and we'd get evicted for nonpayment.
I never saw the four seasons change from the same apartment. During
one move, we couldn't fit an oval 1970s couch past the turn in the stairs.
My sister and I struggled on one end, my dad on the other. Fed up, he
sawed off the back center leg. When we finally got it inside, Dad used
three of Mom's larger books to act as feet for the couch. "Don't tell your
mother," he said. We'd laugh. We never understood why she saved them.
They seemed like deadweight.

Each move, I double-stacked bookcases into tiny apartments, one on

30

top of the other, then double-stacked the books onto the shelves while Mom and Dad went to the old apartment to clean up. Gina, my sister, was only ten months older than I was. We were as close in age as two siblings could get without being twins. One time, when we were about seven or eight, my parents were both out for the day. Gina climbed a set of book-cases like a ladder to reach something on top, and then she and both bookcases tumbled to the floor. She wasn't even scratched. I yelled at her as we rushed to replace the books in haphazard order before our parents came home. Mom never noticed, and if she did, she never said anything.

Move after move, I boxed, carried, unpacked, and re-shelved hundreds of authors—Faulkner, Twain, Kafka, Miller, Crane, Baldwin, Swift, and Dante. My mother had a complete box set of Hemingway novels. I always put them on the shelf by size starting with *The Old Man and the Sea* and ending with *For Whom the Bell Tolls*. I held those books so many times, their authors and titles were imprinted in my mind before I ever knew their importance. Red crayon covered the front of Faulkner's *Go Down Moses*. Inside the yellowed pages, my childlike scribbles superimposed over paragraph-long sentences. My fourth-grade apology—*sorry mom it was a accident*—replaced the torn-off cover of J. D. Salinger's *Catcher in the Rye*.

When I was twenty-seven, I hadn't been thinking about college, but a friend of mine told me it was possible, even then, in the midst of all that scraping and struggling. Gina had been arrested again for prostitution. Mom and Dad had separated by then, but they still spent most of their time together. The three of us lived in separate studio apartments within blocks of each other. Dad would call me up two days before payday and ask for money. "Angie," he'd say in that Boston accent, "your mother and I need some money for cigarettes and food." I'd scrounge up six dollars in change for them. The next week, I'd ask one of them for money to buy a loaf of bread and carton of eggs to last a couple days. There was no reason to think I could go to school, but my friend took me to the community college's registration office, then he held my hand at the financial aid office. He told me I could figure it out, and if I couldn't, I had nothing to lose.

I couldn't afford textbooks that first year. Whatever readings weren't at the library or online, I read in the aisles of the bookstore. In my Modern American Literature class, I was assigned a list of titles I hadn't thought about since I moved out of my parents' house. So one night, I bought a few groceries and boarded the bus to mom's studio apartment.

While waiting for dinner in my mother's tight-walled living room, I looked over at her bookcases, the ones I had stacked again and again over the years. The books, tidy-wedged on polished shelves, stood as testament to her love of books. They competed for space with the TV, a stereo, her brown plaid pullout couch, and two twittering canaries in antique cages.

"Mom, did you really read all of those books?"

"When I was in the state hospital. There was not much to do but sit in the dayroom," she said as she flipped the chicken legs in the pan. "You can read a lot of books in twelve years, Angie."

In the back of my mind, a switch flipped. I had always thought those books just filled space in Mom's shoddy memory. I never believed she'd actually read them. But now I saw past all of her dark paranoia-induced rages, all my childhood years: the tantrums at the grocery store because someone looked at her wrong; the repeating and rocking and swearing because she saw herself backed into a corner; the embarrassment I felt at school, on the bus, in my own living room. I picked up Kafka's *The Trial*, fingered the creases on the binder, turned the yellowed pages, skeptical. "What's this about?"

"You can read it if you want. It's kind of strange. This guy is on trial and you never find out why. Maybe you can make sense of it."

I saw her reading it in the corner of her hospital ward as a teen, her feet up over the side of a cushioned chair, other patients milling about, crayoned drawings of golden moons and pink-gilded princesses on the wall, the sun shining in from a barred window behind her, her dreaming of boys and high school dances that she would never experience. She went into the hospital in eighth grade and did not come out until she met my father on the ward and got married at twenty-six. They only lasted a couple years, long enough to have my sister and me before he started drinking and raging again. She sought refuge at the AA meetings, where she knew my father would not show up again. That's where she met my stepdad, John.

I asked Mom if I could borrow *Huckleberry Finn* and *The Red Badge of Courage*. I located them on the shelves while she mashed potatoes. I saw the Hemingways in the same order I had arranged them as a child. I pulled out *The Old Man and the Sea* and held it like a gem. I had learned by then, those titles were classics. "Mom, have you read all of these Hemingway books?"

"Yeah, do you want to take one? Don't start with that. It's about an old fisherman. I didn't like it. It's slow. Read *A Farewell to Arms*: it's a beautiful love story and it has a young hunk in it."

I took them both.

Later that week, I went to the park across the street from my own tight-walled studio. I had a few hours to breathe some air and sit in the sun after work and before my evening class. Though I didn't need it for school, I pulled out *The Old Man and the Sea* and read it in one sitting. The next week, I read *A Farewell to Arms*. Later, I read Kafka, Miller, Woolf, and Baldwin. In class, we went over that beautiful opening in the first paragraph of James Baldwin's "Sonny's Blues." The word "it" is repeated six times. At first, the "it" refers to the story in the newspaper where the narrator learns his brother, Sonny, was arrested for heroin. But then sentence by sentence, the "it" changes. "It" becomes representative of the struggle the brothers experience, of all things visible and invisible, of black and white. Then the "it" evolves into something even larger as it dangles in the "swinging lights of the subway car, and in the faces and the bodies of the people." By the end of the paragraph, he sees the "it" in his "own face trapped in the darkness which roared outside." I couldn't stop thinking about that physical image—the narrator seeing his own reflection in the subway window—about how both the light inside and that backdrop of darkness outside were necessary in order for him to reflect upon his own image, his own life, and what it meant to him.

Then my mother called me up one morning and said, "Your dad died at the VA Hospital last night. Can you figure out the details?" I called the VA, and they said everything was taken care of and did I want a service? I said no. But I took the day off school and drove the two hours alone to the cemetery to watch from a distance as they interred the coffin. We just went on about our lives after that.

By the time I was in grad school, something triggered mom's paranoia again, and she was evicted from her apartment. It had started with mom calling 911 daily about some threat in her apartment. Other times it was her neighbors who called 911 on her. It got so the 911 operators had my number on file whenever a call came in for my mother's address. One hot August night, I received a phone call.

"Angie Stevens? This is the 911 operator calling about Carole Foster—is that your mother?"

"Yes, she's my mother."

"Several of her neighbors have called about her again. She's on her front porch swearing and threatening people who walk by. We wanted to call you first to see if you can calm her down. If not, we'll have to mental health arrest her."

She lived in Rochester's young, hip Park Avenue area. It was within walking distance to a bus stop and near everything that could make her self-sufficient without a car. When I arrived at the apartment, it was well after midnight. She was on her front porch waving a frantic fist. Her nipples poked through a sheer nightgown. Sweat dripped down her red face as she screamed. Neighbors sat theater style sneering on their porches across the street.

"Fuck you motherfuckers! I'll roll up the sky on you—who the fuck do you think you are? GO AHEAD! CALL THE MOTHERFUCKING POLICE! I'll tell them how you threatened me!"

"MOM! Stop!" I grabbed hold of her clammy arms and forced her inside the house and up the stairs. She smelled of cigarettes and diarrhea.

Her lunatic repeating unnerved me that late at night, all those people staring at us. "Those motherfuckers—who do they think they are? He told me he would roll up the sky! Roll up the fucking sky! I don't care if I get arrested, Angie. I don't care. I don't care. I don't care."

"Mom, I didn't hear them say anything; you're the one screaming." I was raging inside. "Shut the fuck up; nobody is coming after you," I wanted to say. But instead, I grabbed a towel and threw it at her. "Jesus, mom, you've got to find a way to calm down; no one is going to do anything to you. Wipe your face." I leaned against the chair and mumbled, "Roll up the sky? What does that even mean?"

"Angie, I heard them. I heard them. I heard them. They were on the other side of that bedroom wall screaming, 'I'll roll up the world.'" She wailed my name, like a child's whine stretching out the second syllable so it sounded like angeeee. Her mad pacing back and forth across the tiny living room was so unnatural it made me cringe.

"There's nothing out there, Mom. It's an outside wall of a second floor." I took her by the arm and walked her to her chair and made her sit.

"I've got to work tomorrow. I can't be coming over here at all hours of the night. You need to stay calm." Then I kissed on her cheek and walked out. On the stairs, in a whisper, I spat, "God, I fucking hate . . . her."

Two weeks later, she got an eviction notice. I took over. I found another apartment around the corner in the same neighborhood. I borrowed a truck and asked my friend JJ if she would help me. JJ and I had been roommates for years, and as my best friend, she knew Mom well. She also had a patience for my mother that I could not for the life of me summon.

In the past, Mom had always seemed to know when her sickness meant she couldn't decipher reality anymore and it was time to admit herself to the psych center. I guess I thought she would get better on her own or she'd just admit herself when she was ready, but maybe I had been wrong all those years. Maybe it was really Dad who had always made the decision.

One year after Mom had been admitted again—Gina and I were around twelve and thirteen—Dad had gone to visit Mom in the state hospital. She asked him to bring her some vampire books. He brought her *Salem's Lot* and *Frankenstein*.

"Dad, you know Frankenstein isn't a vampire."

"It's close enough," he said.

When he came home that night, he told us that she had broken her wrist chasing him down the hallway. I imagined her crying on her bed in psych ward, unable to turn the pages of her books. I asked my dad that night why he married her. I couldn't remember a time when they weren't spinning out of control in the same cycle—he would be sober for months, then drunk for weeks; she'd be sort of normal for a while, then psychosis would send her back into paranoia rages.

"Because I loved your mother. She was beautiful when I met her. You two were just babies. We needed each other then. We still do." I tried to recall moments of tenderness between them—Sunday afternoon drives when Mom's play fighting made him laugh, evenings when she rubbed salve on his cracked hands—but most of the time, it was Mom's blood-curdling screams and his swearing that pervaded our lives.

The day that JJ and I were supposed to move Mom, we tried to be strategic. Transfer Mom and enough comfortable things in the first trip to the new apartment so that she wouldn't bother us with her tirades while we worked. She smelled like she hadn't showered in days; vagina, urine, and smoke seeped through her clothes. I wanted to put a plastic bag on the seat before she got into the truck. We decided to bring her TV, some food, a couch and table, all of her bath stuff and clean clothes so she could take a shower while we moved another load. I put on a pot of coffee, and JJ hung a new shower curtain. We plugged in the TV and set up the couch and table across from it. As bare as it was, with the coffee going and the television on, it felt like a home. We left her in the shower so we could move another load.

JJ and I were already halfway through packing a second load when we heard the screaming outside. Mom's faint voice coming from down the road stopped us both. JJ and I looked at each other and ran down the stairs. Outside, we heard her, "Angeeeee, oh God," she yelled. She was running toward us from her new apartment less than a block away, naked, holding a small towel by its corner barely covering a breast. I heard a neighbor whisper, "Oh, my God" as we ran to meet her. JJ on one side, me on the other, we held the towel in front of her as we rushed her to the porch and up the stairs. "Oh God, Oh God, Thank God you're safe, Angie!" she cried.

"Mom, of course I'm safe. What did you think happened?"

"I heard the thunder when I was in the shower, and I could have sworn someone shot you. I thought someone was shooting you, Angeee."

Later, when the police came to take her, she wasn't having any of it. She pleaded with me not to send her away. The cops held her arms. She kicked and screamed, "Let go of me."

"It's ok, Mom. I'll pack up some books for you and some clothes. I'll come visit. It will get better," I said. But I didn't know that for sure. I wasn't seeing things clearly. I don't think I would have called 911 that day. It was JJ who said it was time to call the police. I might have otherwise just tried to wait it out, let Mom get mental health arrested by someone else when I wasn't around. I had never had to be the one to make that call before.

In graduate school, I read twenty books a semester. I took a class called Readers as Writers, where we studied post-modernism. I fell in love with Dave Eggers' *A Heartbreaking Work of Staggering Genius*. There's the scene where he throws his mother's ashes into the ocean. It's supposed to be reverent and melancholy, but he's working against the wind. The ashes fly back into his face and in his mouth, and he's cursing himself for spitting out his mother. I read that scene in prayer style, knees on the floor, the book held open on the bed in my one-room studio; and I alternated between heaving sobs and choking laughter.

I saw my mom and her years in the asylum—all of her stories, setting fire to a maintenance closet because her doctor wouldn't reciprocate her love, feeling the electrodes pulse against her temples as a teenager, and even later, falling in love with my biological father, Reggie, who was on the ward for alcoholism, both of them getting discharged to start a new life outside those walls. I imagined her packing into boxes, for the first time, the books that lined her hospital room. They were the only things she could call her own. That collection grew as the years passed until it dominated everything else in our home, until it became the only consistency in our lives. I realized then that carrying her books all those years had only made me stronger.

My mother died the year I started graduate school. With an oxygen line in her nose, she lit a cigarette. The line caught fire and burned everything in its path from the living room where she sat all the way along the floor to her bedroom where the fire stopped at the failsafe on the oxygen tank. She tamped the growing fire down with a towel while crawling on her knees from room to room. But she was too slow. The smoke filled her lungs, and she passed out just after she had put the fire out. She had a heart attack when she arrived at the hospital.

Gina sobered up for the weeks after my mother's death; the crack-pipe blisters on her fingers healed, and she seemed normal for a while. We drove together to Mom's apartment the day we received the ashes. Most of my mother's belongings went to the curb. We left the big furniture behind. Neither of us had room, so we told the maintenance man to give it away. I brought plastic totes for the things we would keep: old pictures of our grandmother, who had died in a fireworks factory when our mother was eight months old; our mother's wedding band with the little lightning bolt on it; a few pictures of us when we were girls; the crystal glasses our mother had saved for years to buy and then left preserved in boxes for most of our lives; the red and white blanket she crocheted; and her books.

Gina walked across the street to get us hamburgers for lunch, and I sat on the floor in front of the bookshelves and wept. Most of the books were damaged beyond repair. Some were over fifty years old. I put them in the recycle bin for the curb. Then I found Salinger's *Catcher in the Rye*. I wiped off the dust and placed it neatly into an empty box. I cleaned off the Hemingways one at a time starting with *The Old Man and the Sea* and ending with *For Whom the Bell Tolls* and packed them away into the box too, then Faulkner, Twain, Kafka, Miller, Crane, Baldwin, Swift, and Dante, and a few others. Later that afternoon, I lugged that box up the stairs to my own tiny studio. I put it in the living room, where the sun's rays slanted across the carpet. I opened the box, and beginning with *The Old Man and the Sea*, I placed the books on the shelves, one by one, next to my own collection.

# Household Idols

AVI STEINBERG

When I was a baby, my father spent his days at the university, reading philosophy and plugging away at his dissertation, and my mother worked across town, in western Jerusalem, at the zoo. Her job was to feed and tend the cockatiels, who uttered their Hebrew quips with slightly off-kilter Israeli accents. *MahNeeshmaa BohhkerTov BohhkerTov Shabbatshalom.* For my parents, American-raised immigrants in Jerusalem, this was a kind of utopia. They were young seekers, religious bohemians, and Vietnam War—era dropouts, and this extended pilgrimage in the Holy Land was the fulfillment not only of the ancient hopes of their Jewish faith but also of their own families' deepest desires. Their parents, refugees from Eastern Europe, loved the U.S. because it had saved their lives. But as pious Jews, they viewed their children's immigration to Jerusalem as a lifelong dream—the kind of dream in which even the birds speak in God's holy tongue.

As it turned out, this sojourn in the Holy City was temporary, undone by life things: my parents' growing disenchantment with Israeli society and distance from aging parents. In retrospect, it was just one stop in my parents' wanderings. They'd met in kindergarten and were more or less married from then on. They shared a desire to leave St. Louis, albeit for different reasons: my father was fleeing the stifling comforts of post—World War II suburban complacency, and my mother was escaping a physically and emotionally abusive upbringing. They've never quite stopped moving since, their life made of geographic sequels and second acts and occasional non sequiturs. There was Boston, New York, Jerusalem, Cleveland, Boston again, and finally, as of this writing, Berkeley, California.

But my parents' golden age, the emotional pole around which all travel revolves, has been and will always be Jerusalem. They are believers, after all. Today, even as they've made a home in California, as geographically distant from the Holy City as they've ever lived, the walls of their house are covered with art from and about Jerusalem. The farther they've moved from it, the more art of Jerusalem they accumulate. These images, in paintings and etchings and carvings and paper cuts, are mostly not iconic biblical or religious scenes but smaller and more personal, lyric turns: homes in familiar neighborhoods, the lighting and color moods of the place. All in romantic tones. Echoes, big and small, of the famous line of medieval Hebrew poet Yehuda Ha-Levi (the namesake of my sister's elementary school in Jerusalem): *My heart is in the east, and I in the outermost west.* This Jerusalem collection is the permanent exhibit in my parents' home, the official family legend.

But there's also a variety of ever-shifting exhibits that belong to my mother alone, sprung from her private world. She manages a growing number of small installations, an evolving series of tableaux drawn from her own collections and, from what I can tell, deep in her soul. These are little figurines, sculptures, found scraps, and rare bits and bobs of all kinds. She had at one point, for instance, a small collection of wooden toys, mostly on wheels, that once served as her children's playthings. On my thirtieth birthday, she'd pointed to a tiny wooden train, delicate and barely holding together, and told me, "I got this one for you when you were born." I couldn't help feel that she was saying, "Look at this worn, but not worn-out thing: this is what thirty years looks like." She had a collection of teeeeny-tiny books and equally tiny writing implements—wee pens and colored pencils—that presumably belonged in the even teeny-tinier hands of the human and animal figures nearby, and that were highly suggestive of the artistic visions that lived inside their teeny-tiny heads. She would cultivate separate collections—colorful stones and minerals from around the world—and equally colorful action figures, partly for the sake, it seemed, of crossing these worlds for dramatic effect: showing, for instance, a small cowboy effortlessly hoisting one of her stones, or else, as the mood might take her, weighed down, or beset on all sides by these rocks. A smattering of metallic family kiddush cups, used for ritual purposes, has, in her care, morphed into a sprawling collection that she has "rescued"—her word—from the antiques stores of the gentiles. The unifying factors in her collections are that almost all items are antiques, all are visually interesting and colorful and, most of all, carefully arranged, often in tellingly narrative ways. Every gesture and turn of a figure's head or arm seems somehow significant.

My mother's tableaux, to me, stand as a challenge or complicating factor in the Jerusalem narrative told through the family's official art collection. Because I was raised inside the old Jewish sagas, I happen to know that this dynamic of an official (patriarchal) cult challenged by a quieter but persistent domestic (matriarchal) cult dates back to biblical times: In and around almost every story in the Hebrew Bible are echoes of the patriarchal worship of one single Male Sky God—sometimes known as Yahweh, other times as "the Lord," who has his home in Jerusalem—struggling to assert itself over the private religions practiced in the home, mostly by women, who didn't have much use for the boys' club of Jerusalem politics. This female cult, a veneration of household gods and small idols and fetishes, often involved goddess worship.

If you pay attention, you see it all over the story. It's there, at the beginning, in the Book of Genesis, when Rachel—the mother of Israel herself!—is caught trying to sneak out some little household idols, which she'd secreted under her camel saddle. When she's asked to stand up so that her bag can be searched by the patriarchs of the house, she replies slyly, "Don't be angry, sir, that I cannot stand up: I am having my period." Our text doesn't describe mother Rachel's inward grin, but I believe it's strongly implied.

Much later in the Hebrew Bible, the prophets rant against the folk practices of household idol worship, especially those that depict the

Semitic goddess Asherah. Those biblically bearded men hate and fear Asherah in ways that can only be described as maniacal, and it is this deeply paranoid misogyny that fires their own cultic beliefs and practices. In the Ten Commandments, the number one and two dictates are against "having other gods" and against making graven images of these gods. At various moments in the biblical saga, the people of Israel are told to smash any and all idols that they can get their hands on. If there's any doubt about the gendered nature of these commandments, the male God likes to describe himself as a jealous husband and derides the veneration of Asherah as a form of harlotry.

The vehemence behind these commandments suggests that the norm, in fact, was in the breach. The goddess Asherah and her female followers, who must have been quite a group, could never really be suppressed. On the contrary, they seemed to thrive. This never ceased to vex the male prophets, who famously described their hated rival as maddeningly present "on every high hill and under every green tree." That phrasing itself is ubiquitous, used in seven different biblical books and sometimes more than once. It was supposed to be an indictment, but of course, it's actually a grudging compliment to the popularity of the goddess and to the devotion of her acolytes. Modern archaeology has confirmed all of this: the biblical heartland is positively full of little idols.

Something like this conflict, writ small, seems to play itself out in my family home, where my mother's private practices, her figurines and their private meanings, quietly carve out their own space within the cult of Jerusalem, which has always been more my father's thing. (The purchasing of that Jerusalem art, like the decision to move to Jerusalem all those years ago, came at my father's behest.) Growing up, and largely a product of my upbringing in the world of Orthodox Judaism, I tended toward the patriarchal cult of Jerusalem. As a fervent believer, I did what Orthodoxy asked of me: three times a day I turned my body and physically faced Jerusalem, regardless of where I stood in the world, and I recited prayers about Jerusalem. But as I got older, I gravitated to where my heart really was: with my mother's quieter cultic practice, her menageries of household idols. It's a discovery that was comforting because it was an arrival at a truth. It was also troubling for exactly the same reason.

I didn't make the discovery alone. My sister, Adena, who finds these collections unsettling, not long ago walked into my apartment after having not visited for a long time. When she saw the kinds of things that had gathered on my shelves—the old board game pieces, mixed up and rearranged, the antique stereoscope slides, the collections of multicolored zippers—she'd stopped short, given me a look expressive of true horror, and exclaimed, "Omigod, are you Roz?" There was a sense of betrayal in my sister's comment, as if she were saying, "Are you of that persuasion? Are you like our troubled mother, the one we complain about, the one whose troubling presence in our lives is part of *our* bond?" I think my sister felt somewhat abandoned, as though she were now suddenly left alone in her struggle to process our mother and, most of all, to not become our mother.

I'd had a similar shock myself. Around this same period, I'd visited my parents' home in Berkeley and discovered that my mother's collection of antique tins, which once held cookies or sardines or tobacco, not only resembled mine, color for color, but that it was nearly identically displayed, and that she had placed figurines, who could be twins with mine, in tandem with the tins, and in nearly identical poses. There was one little guy, sitting with his back against one tin, and a critter hiding with only his head peeking out behind another. Two others who were shaking hands/paws. I don't know whether Asherah or some other authority on high had secretly decreed these arrangements, but it might as well have been so, they were that identical.

This discovery came rather late, considering that we'd long shared the impulse for collecting. When I was a child, my mother conferred her blessings onto my collection efforts. Though not a sports fan, she immediately grasped the import of my baseball card collection. Always she encouraged it, actively aiding me in my endless searches by kindly chauffeuring me to rural corners of Ohio for sports cards shows, long drives from our home in Cleveland Heights. She helped me subscribe to the trade magazines, even to *Beckett*, which listed the monthly dollar values of these cards like a stock sheet (violating her strongly held principles of collecting free of profit motive). Even before this era of baseball cards, we'd been going to collection shows, mostly of the rock and gem variety; it was a passion of hers that I'd taken to immediately.

My mother's rocks and driftwoods, bird nests and blanched coral, and such, gave my long-suffering sister the heebie-jeebies. The inorganic collections just depressed her. What did Roz see in a collection of old, broken-down mechanical devices? My sister, a shrink by training, is still reluctant to plumb those morbid depths. Of one of these devices, an old clock that we encountered in an antiques shop, and that appeared to have been attacked and thoroughly done in by some sort of blunt object, my sister told me, "It just bums me out, to be honest. It's *broken*." But my mother, of course, was contemplating dropping a largish sum for this pile of clock parts, even though it was broken. In fact, precisely because of its brokenness—of the elaborate and abjectly vulnerable transparency of that brokenness, the surprising peek it offered into a world of super tiny little widgets from the Edwardian period, so precious and unexpected, and meaningful because, you know, Time, and because of the way in which this clock pile had randomly but rather elegantly arranged itself into an organic sculpture—my mother saw and cherished it, and I, too, recognized it as beautiful.

But my sister had a point: This thing could justly be described as mere junk, clutter. Where would it plausibly live in my parents' house? Displaying garbage in a home isn't a sign of good health. It can be bad for morale. For my sister, and for me, growing up among such pieces was often a painful experience. This sense of brokenness too closely matched the actual living situation in our home—my mother's depression, the ghosts of her childhood, and her struggles to cope, all while running a house and raising us, and never quite figuring out how to do any of that efficiently, nor figuring out how to launch a career, and all while dealing with mounting health problems. Money was often short and financial decision-making incompetent. There was a baseline of existential anxiety.

The prolonged search for a couch once turned into a Melvillian saga that almost undid the fabric of our family. My father was out doing his academic hustle and not particularly helpful at home, and my mother was left to do house management while also working as a nanny. This situation, which would be difficult for anyone, was often doubly or triply so for my mother because she lacked some basic skills. My mother spent her formative years in fear of her mother's emotional abuse and her father's physical abuse: the lessons were in survival, in getting by, not in how to thrive or cultivate safe and happy spaces.

Years later, (after Jerusalem and after Cleveland), my parents made the decision to live in a basement apartment in the Boston area, because it was a more affordable way to live in a nice neighborhood in Cambridge. And when this place started regularly flooding, inundated by nearly a foot-deep pool of water in the living room during major storms, it was clear to us kids that our house was reverting into a musty cellar, that there was nothing to be done. It was our Fate. House repairs were always behind the curve, and despite occasional nods to modernity, the place felt as though it might fall apart at any minute. Because the home in which these tableaux were displayed did not feel secure and had become slightly smelly and a tad depressing, my sister has always felt understandably triggered by the collections, or what she sometimes called "the wood chunks."

To me, it's more painful that my mother has such a keen eye for design. There's a poignancy in my mother's artful touches, in her way of splurging on gorgeously lush peonies and arranging them beautifully atop some crummy ledge that might be permanently waterlogged and rotted from within. This adorning of ruins has always been emotionally fraught for me and my sister, especially with my mother's tragic habit of bringing up, often while arranging these artifacts, all the career paths she should have taken instead of being a nanny. There was the zoo, of course, but that was just a lark. In Jerusalem in the 1970s, you could get a job at the zoo if you ran into a zookeeper on a bus and made friends with him. Later, in Cleveland, she'd briefly trained as a real estate agent. But nothing came of it.

She would talk about her time working as a children's librarian in South Boston in the late sixties, a story that often ended with, "I should have been a children's librarian." Other careers she should have pursued: editor at a children's literary imprint, curator in a museum, anthropologist. Field biologist. Florist. Designer. An artist of some sort. Her family was full of artists, of all persuasions and modes and levels of success, from struggling novelists to the drummer of Jane's Addiction and the founding designer of Hanky Panky lingerie. All are her cousins. But my mother never had the confidence to chase her own dreams, at least not in the form of a career. Something about her assemblage of regrets, of unfilled dreams—a collection that my mother seems to dust off and tend to fairly often in conversation—is strongly associated, in my mind, with her actual collections. The intention and care given to her objects somehow testifies to her thwarted ambitions, and it can be painful to witness. I understand my sister's discomfort.

But unlike my sister, I also happen to share my mother's passion for collecting. This complicates matters for me. Whereas my sister pretty much hates it all and resents the painful feelings it evokes, I delight in the make-believe, and the freedom that comes with that playfulness.

But feelings of guilt tend to spoil that fun. I can't but catch myself and wonder about the joy of collecting: is it really joyous? Or is it a sign of stuntedness, even pathology, a form of evasion, of escapism? Is this a childlike enthusiasm or just childishness? I may never know the answer. But this much is clear: the semi-compulsion to collect artifacts, and to collect, too, their complicated meanings, is my main inheritance from my mother.

In case there's any doubt that it's an actual inheritance, my mother often reminds me of it. She'll pick up a piece and say to me, "Now this one . . . he's *all yours*." She loves this line. That refrain, that something is *all yours*, has become a private joke between us. It's funny because it's painfully true. Any time my mother acquires a piece of picturesque junk, she introduces it to me with this performance, a curious blend of pride and self-effacement. With a touch of defensiveness, she extols the new acquisition's virtues, including that primary one: "It's really old." Authenticity, denoted by age, is nonnegotiable with my mother.

When I visit, my mother usually reveals some newly acquired folksy artifact, often an antique piece of Americana. Recently, she showed me a clunky wood-sculptured cowboy on a bucking bronco, about the height and weight of midsized fire extinguisher. Every detail seems off, but in the way it's so consistently, thoroughly wrong, it somehow becomes interesting, unique. Most people would look at it and, correctly, declare it "ugly," or even hideous, and walk by.

"Isn't it bizarre?" she told me. "Adena would hate it. I just had to have it. And look," she said, showing me the deep, irregular grooves in the horse's mane, apparently made by someone's knife, "you can tell that it's handmade. The wood is really cool. Feel it . . ."

She handed it to me and watched for my reaction. This thing was like a brick. What kind of wood was this: Verawood, ironwood? I smiled. She smiled.

"Heavy, right? I just love it."

She loves this clunky wood-sculptured cowboy. But she also expresses her slight guilt and anxiety, knowing that the piece is an indulgence, a waste of money and space and, eventually, another burden to me—a guilt deepened because she knows I'm also feeling all kinds of feelings about it. "Well," she says, putting the household idol back in its carefully appointed spot, "when the time comes, it's all yours, *boychik*."

She laughs to herself, but her look is mostly of regret. All of which I register immediately and can feel squeezing, in a literal, bodily way, at my heart. The joke of *it's all yours* also hints at a deeper sadness: that this may really be it, legacy-wise. That my parents, despite their hopes, aren't leaving me or my sister with any inheritance. Unlike what my father's father managed to accomplish at the end of his life—his successful career as a supermarket owner—my parents will leave no land, no assets, nor, probably, any cash to help with the future. There may even be debts. Worse than that, there may not be enough for my parents' own long retirement, a scary prospect for all of us. My mother's artfully collected junk really might be all there is. My sister can barely tolerate looking at it. It's all yours, *boychik*!

For my mother, there's sadness and shame in all of this. But my mom is a humorist, especially when things get dark. And what can I say? I'm my mother's son: if your legacy is a pile of antique sardine tins, it's probably best to have a sense of humor about it. For me, humor itself is part of that legacy.

But what the collections are most essentially about is communication: they are, for my mother, a way of communicating with parts of herself, and of communicating these parts of herself to others, to those who have the eyes to see it. There have been times, I believe, that my mother conveyed specific messages to me solely through her figurines. One time, I'd visited after what had been a very difficult period for her. She'd had major health scares. Finances continued to be a source of stress. The depression had deepened and made doing anything to help herself exponentially more difficult. I hadn't visited in a while, nor been in good touch. When I arrived, many of her little animals had taken a decidedly downcast attitude. Heads were bowed, tails were curled up, all were seated and drawn inward. But on the second day of my stay, after we'd had some quality time together and my mother's spirits lifted, I suddenly noticed that all of the little critters had brightened considerably: They were standing with tails at attention, or they were running in suspended motion. One had assumed a lovely balletic fourth position. I doubt this was my doing alone, or a message for me alone. But I also know that my mother knew I would notice. She was thanking me for my role in cheering her up. She was telling me that she loved me and that things would be okay.

In this way, the little figurines are truly holy to me. As the medium—a kind of emotional oracle—by which my mother can access a part of herself, the scary and delicate parts, and express them, these objects make up a kind of sacred household practice, far more divine than any tower in Jerusalem.

As I consider having a child of my own now, I can't help but wonder about passing on this compulsion for collecting to another person. Will

I, one day, lumber through my mounting tchotchkes, pick up a quirky brick-heavy thing and shake it at some other poor soul, whom I created, and say to her, "It's all yours, kiddo!" Is that how this goes?

I'm not sure what I'll decide. Will I continue my mother's veneration of household idols, or not? Probably I'll dither for years and change my policy a few times. But if I had to make a prediction, I'd say it's pretty likely that a kid of mine (and of my partner, who is also very much prone to collections and miniatures) will inherit this legacy. Probably I will continue to cultivate these collections—which doesn't necessarily mean to expand them, because culling them, too, is part of the curatorial project—because collecting, for me, is a way to be honest. It isn't just about honoring my mother but about communicating the part of me that is the way it is, and can be no other way, because of my mother. I hope it's a legacy that gives some joy to its next owner, and if not, that it's at least manageably lightweight enough to fit into one sensible moving box.

# Just Say the Word

LIZZIE SKURNICK

I remember when my son first told me my name. We were standing in the foyer, about to walk up the stairs. "You're *Lizzie*," he said, as if he'd suddenly been let in on some terrific joke.

My mother had had a particularly difficult time with my using a sperm donor. She had been born in 1945, and so I didn't think this was surprising—only hated to speak to her about it. When we did talk, her face and voice took on a strained look, as if she were apologizing for something she couldn't control.

I also remember the first time Javi spoke directly to me. We were leaving the house, and as I got in the back of the car, he turned to me from his car seat. "Hi, Mom," he said.

As is often the case when someone apologizes, I can't remember how my mother did. I think it might have been that there was nothing wrong with me, or nothing wrong with the baby-to-be, or nothing wrong with having a baby without a man, or realizing it had nothing to do with a man at all. It's possible it was all of these.

Dearest Lizzie,

I regret talking, over Christmas dinner yet!, about your plan to be a mother. I apologize to you. I am furious with myself. Nobody ever said anything dissuasive to me about getting pregnant. That you want to be a mother is a blessing. There is nothing wrong with your wish or your plans. I want to be in them fully.

I love you,
Mom

The first time Javi spoke at all was in a public bathroom. I turned from the changing table and heard someone utter a loud "Hi!" I looked at the blonde lady at the sink. "Did *he* say that?" I asked her.

After Javi was born, my mother suddenly began to talk about everyone as if she were giving them a eulogy. ". . . and she tried hard, and it worked, and it was good for her," she would trail off, or finish, ". . . and that was what happened, and it was fine." Then, she would attempt to smile.

Dear Lizzie I have been not getting in touch with you reprehensibly. But I intend to be much better, as I want to know what he looks like. I think he must be bouncy, hungry, and handsome. Stay well and full of energy. I love you, Lovely. Love, Mom

For years, my mother had called me once a month with the same strain in her voice. I would say, "Mom, if you don't want to talk on the phone, we don't have to talk," and she would say with relief, "I don't, daughter. Thank you."

The lady said "yes." I took a picture of them together and put it on Facebook.

One day I pulled a journal out of my bookcase—a red book of blank pages someone had given me titled *My Quotable Kid*. By then, Javi was three, and it seemed like maybe that was too late.

My mother also used to send me another kind of email, early in the morning. *Dear daughter*, it would say. *The sky is blue and the birds are singing and I wish a glorious day on you. Dear daughter, when I woke this morning I thought of you and your glorious beauty*. They unaccountably filled me with rage. "Mom, stop sending me these!" I finally said.

Dearest Lizzie,

I was thinking about you yesterday, because you were going to leave for LA today, and that fact notwithstanding, and the equally unsettling fact that huge rains were forecast for yesterday, which I was afraid to drive in, I was at work and driving from one patient to another, and was led by my GPS to Bronx Parkway or Bronx Highway, which I did not recall ever being on, or even ever hearing about. It turned out to be an old, serpiginous two-lane highway, gloriously without any traffic at all, which wound through Garth Forest, a name typical for stone-bastioned Wealthy Westchester, of Pelhams, and Chatsworths and Saxon Woods and endless avenues named for one syllable trees of the northern hemisphere—Oak Ave, Beech Ave, etc. Anyway, the staid, Anglo Garth Forest made me think of your true observation that the names for towns and streets in Baltimore are all random inspirations recalling nothing known. Garth Forest itself was truly beautiful, and well-named: all the trees were very tall and just bursting into leaf, and as I was driving through it, the sun lit up the light green at the tops. And a wide rushing brook came near the highway twice. But the winding of it made me think of the only time I can remember you ever vomiting, which was when we were driving up the continually winding road leading to a volcano in Hawaii, you, barely a year old, in my lap. It was the right thing to do. You always absorb your setting and have an apt response.

I love you,

In the sperm donor's information packet, he says he's asked his mother what he liked to do as a child. She can't remember much, but she does remember that he liked to look at huge industrial fans.

When I next saw my mother, she looked sad. "Lizzie, you can't tell a person how to write to you," she said quietly. And she was right.

Dear Javi: You liked to roll cars slowly along the couch and look at their wheels. You liked to slit your eyes to the side and turn around and around to watch the way the world slid by. You watched the fan so often I started to call you "My friend, fan." When you were a newborn, I pushed the cat away from you because I was worried he would smother you, and he went and hid in his carrier for two days.

Is it that children loom so large for you—keeping them alive, feeding them, making them talk, making them be quiet, reading to them, avoiding painting with them, painting with them—that there is no room but for the present moment, and its shame and anxiety?

My poor mother. She had to take me to violin every Monday night from the time I was seven, and we both hated it. Now that I think about it, probably the teacher did too, and so did her son, who did his home-work in the living room while she taught me on the side porch and my mother sat on the couch. It would have been six o'clock. Afterward, we went to a diner, where I would have Hawaiian Ham, which was slices of deli ham and canned pineapple covered with maple syrup.

For instance, this week, I found out I have to attend dance with Javi, because he jumps off the stage and runs around the room and they are worried about the liability.

That my mother let me order this meal seems to me a great act of love.

You only know what your child actually does from what other people say about him. What people say about Javi is that he is hyper-verbal. On the elevator, they ask, impressed, How old is he? And each time someone hasn't seen him, they say, He talks so well!

Your grandmother is a doctor, and she knew what it was when you pulled one arm as if you were about to fire an arrow. "That's the fencing reflex," she said. It's an important developmental stage.

Somewhere in this week's *New England Journal of Medicine* or in *JAMA*, an enterprising group has published their findings in a huge study of pre-pregnant Norwegian women who were taking folic acid, became pregnant, continued taking folic acid, during their pregnancies, especially in the first 6–8 weeks of pregnancy when the fetal brain cells are developing, and gave birth to infants who had a 40% decrease in autism, at least the milder forms, like Asperger's syndrome. This study is thought to confirm the findings of smaller studies, which had argued a benefit of folic acid in pregnancy and pre-conception in reducing autism, but were too small to draw any conclusions. Since autism is thought to affect 1/100 people on earth, this is a great finding. Folic acid has also been shown to reduce spina bifida in newborns, which is a much rarer disorder. So do ask your doctors, and see what they think. I love you, dear daughter. Love, MOM

I didn't believe my father when he first told me. He said my mother would cling to him at night when they watched TV and she seemed scared. But we all heard her on the phone, prescribing medicines at deafening levels and remembering patients by name.

When I laugh, Javi says, "Mama, why are you funny?" When he smells something, he says, "Mama, what does that smell like?"

But then, you retired, and by the summer, you were calling my brother your brother's name. "Go to your father," you would say to Javi, pointing to my father.

They say "no" so often, someone told me, because that's the word you say most often to them. What Javi says, though, is "No, not!" We have to turn off the TV. "No, not!" It's time to go to bed. "No, not!"

My mother disliked small talk so much that at a party, you would always find her in the corner, talking to the person everyone least liked to talk to.

Then by Thanksgiving, you weren't making any sense at all. At the dinner, you told the two women you hadn't seen in some time that you were having trouble remembering things, and they assured you that they were too. Then, over turkey, you offered a long opinion, and asked, ". . . does that make sense?" One said, "No, can you say more?" and I almost kicked her under the table.

When you were inconsolable, we would hold you up at the kitchen sink and turn on the water. You would quiet suddenly and remain still, except for your left hand, which you would drum up and down the arm of whoever was holding you, like you were keeping a private rhythm.

When my grandmother's dementia got very bad, we would sit and watch *That's Entertainment!* in her living room. She still knew all the songs.

You still know the songs. You sing a falsetto along to every piece of classical music we ever listened to, which I thought you didn't even like.

Finally, some of your friends recognize what is happening. One is a social worker, and she calls to say that we should get you comfortable shoes and put a gate across the stairs. She tells me that she had asked you about my sister. "She was saying a name," her friend says, "but it wasn't your sister's."

Dearest Lady In Waiting,

Like a big Hug, or a big Squeeze, a surprise! But they aren't painful, and that's the second thing you notice, after you note that you haven't quite felt anything like them before. They also feel like the climax ('scuse the term) will gradually build to pain, which they do, but not yet rhythmically. When they get rhythm, they will start to make you hold your breath for the pain you have already begun to feel at their most powerful. The uterus is the strongest muscle in the human body, and it has been practicing for about 9 months, abetted by the acrobatics of its Gift. You can also think that the stronger the squeeze, the shorter the wait. Also Braxton-Hicks do not cause fear. They just cause attention.

Javi insists I count all the steps from our apartment to the door. As the bus whooshes past, he says, "G-R-O-C?" He says, "Mama, what does Frank stand for?"

I tell the doctor that the words my mother makes up sound like a mix of Danish and French. "Did she speak Danish?" the doctor asks with great interest.

Dearest Daughter, at the risk of being entirely mundane, I am happy every day now because this could be the day, or night of. I hope all these preceding Braxton Hicks are smoothing your way, and making for a rapid labor, and I want to be near you. Be hopeful, be happy, and be ready. All my hope is with you.

Love, Mom.

I have been watching *Borgen* and *The Bridge*. I know the Danes say "hvorfor det?" for Why? What for that?

We have to stop the visits because you grab Javi too much. This is not because you're angry but because you're worried—that he will fall, that he is running too fast, that he will fall off the edge. You try to pick him up.

You were born in the following sequence: I was sitting in the house and just thinking, toward dusk, that we should just cross the bridge. I wasn't in labor at all: it was just a thought. So I told Dad we should just cross the bridge. Then when we got across the bridge I was immediately in labor. I think we dropped David off at Grandma Dora's on the way, which Dad said we did. By the time we got to Albert Einstein, which is literally just blocks away, I was really in active labor, so we got out of the car right in front of the high stairs going up a steep hill to the main entrance of Einstein, and we ran up those stairs. When I got to the desk there was a younger woman there just screaming in labor, and I went over to just calm her down, so I couldn't have yet been in the last stages of labor because in that stage you can't do anything but concentrate on getting out of pain in the spaces between contractions and having the baby. But things did go quickly after I told the lady just to take deep breaths, and that it wouldn't hurt so much, when I began to remember how much it did hurt. I was in the room by then and Dr Lewis offered me a pudendal block, which was a needle in the vagina that did stop the pain, and they wheeled me to the delivery room and you were born not that many pushes later. That, I think, was a little after 7pm, August 3, 1973. As you know, Dad was present and thought you were a boy. Dad is polite and would have only glanced. When Dr. Lewis corrected him, he took another quick glance, and said Oh yeah.

Yes indeed. Love,
MomxxxxxxxxxxxxxxxxxxxxxxxxxxxxxxxxxxxxxxxxxxxxxxxxxxxxxxMom,

When someone is black, you have to assure the doctor, *She was a physician. She was an English Professor. She learned German over a summer.*

Though perhaps you need to do this with anyone who isn't anymore what they were.

Javi will not take his fluoride pill without reading the serial numbers they print on each.

At the appointment, I am surprised to see that you cannot identify an igloo. You call a pretzel a bagel. The doctor shows you a picture of interlocking circles. You draw two separate circles. Then she says, "See if you can draw them intersecting." You write in careful script, *Circles intersecting*.

Javi looks up from the changing table and says, "All done!" They say that at the daycare, I realize. The next day, he plops down beside me at the park and says, "I'm too tired to run anymore. I can't do all this running." And that is me.

The doctor asks you to touch her nose. You look at me and my father and draw back, a bit huffy, a bit doubtful. "That's a little . . . rude," you say.

You love the light rail, so we take it a lot. One day, near dark, we are waiting at a terminus for the train to finally leave, when, nervous, I jump out with you to validate the ticket. Immediately, the train dings, and the doors close. I curse and stomp my feet. "Mommy, let's find a station that isn't so . . . damn-y," you say.

Here's a trick all childcare staff use: When they see any parent, they say, "Hi, Mom!"

You and my father used to take Javi to Van Saun Park by yourself, but now I come. This day, you grab Javi, and then you push me. I don't try to make things better, and I take him off and we sit alone, and then Javi asks, "What starts with F?" We do this from A to G, and each time I look desperately around the park to find Ant and Apple and Blue and Bear, I am amazed at what I must be forgetting.

I have taught Javi to say "narrative." This is because I don't want him to only watch trains on YouTube; I want him to watch things with stories. "I want a narrative," he says.

Now, after I am around you, I forget words, often hilariously. "What I discovered is you need to run around to run and sweat off the rosé," I tell my friend, "so you don't get a hamburger." "A hangover?" says my friend. With my mother, the words have some connection to what she is trying to do, but my brain is not trying; it is thinking about something else.

One of our earliest games that my son invented: mouthing the words without talking, as if we're saying something very important.

Dear Lizzie,

I may have told you before that Dad is not the only contributor to your Jewish genes. One of Mama Hebert's grandfathers was a Jewish man, who saw to it that Mama had music lessons. He may be buried in the Jewish cemetery in Donaldsonville, or maybe not, if he was a traveling man. But he was the father of Mama's mother, of whom we now have a picture. It is a stunning photo. She is dressed in full turn-of-the-century dress, with a parasol and a big hat. She is very beautiful, and a quadroon, Carole says. She was a midwife, and she had a nickname, which I am trying to remember.

Love and hugs, Mommy

When we turn on the TV in the middle of the show, Javi says, "The end, the end!" What he wants is the beginning.

Sometimes, the words are not related at all, and it is as if my brain has groped in a drawer and, indifferent, presented the first item it finds. I say "yogurt" for "camp" to some other parents I don't know well and am briefly worried they will think I am drunk, or on drugs.

I am teaching Javi the address of our house. It is 547 Jersey Avenue. Half the time when we say it together, he thinks it's a countdown, and starts 5 · · · 4 · · · 3 · · ·

Another day, I say "lice" instead of "scooter." Am I thinking "lice" because Javi had a tick, and I was thinking about Lyme and telling Javi to be nice? I want it to have that much logic, but if it does, it is an accident.

On the changing table, you say, "Mommy, you said the wrong word! Just say the right word!"

When I was a child, I had a rosy complexion and butter-blond hair. What do you look like—Phylicia Rashad? My father tells the story of the day I was sitting on your lap in the park when another woman leaned across and asked me, "And where is your mother?" According to my father, I looked at her as if she were a nitwit, placed my hand on your thigh, and said, "RIGHT HERE."

Javi asks me for help with the dump truck. I refuse. My mother rises to play with him. "No, you have to," she tells me, "because it farms out a typical slow thing that grows."

Dearest Lizzie, I still can't believe you are about to have a glorious baby all new. This feeling I recognize: when I had Miri I thought everyone was through having kids. When 2 of the women who gave me, a newcomer to their town, who happened to live down the block from one of them, and who already had children of their own, and seemed to be doing it for a reminiscent lark, went on to have more children after I had Miriam, I could never fully grasp it as real, and I still see those children as not adoptions but as adaptations, of the novels their mothers must be composing for all these years. However, Javier is a different story, since he is your baby boy, and thus of us, not a fabrication, but our fabric. My joy is building. It will be amazing seeing us in him, and astounding to see how he is not like us, but himself.
I love you. Get sleep and keep well. I love you, Mom

She looks up from their digging. "Now, where is that green thumb?" she inquires.

*Achille Edward Hebert. Charles Oscar Hebert.* For minutes, my father, mother, and I are equals, trying to remember the full names of her uncles. "I'm trying to think of . . ." my mother says, frustrated, ". . . it's my execution."

One of the best ways I can figure out how my mom is doing it to ask her for help. "Mom, I can't see this letter—can you help me read it?" I try to keep her in sight by asking, "Mom, can you help me with Javi?" This morning I ask if she can help me draw interlocking circles. She writes, *Interlocking circles*.

One morning, Javi points to his door. "Mommy, that was my room because last night I was crying because I wanted you."

We're in the kitchen, reading about Donald Trump and gay marriage in Germany. "The world is moving on without you," I say to Trump's picture. "I thought the world was moving off," Javi says. "Oh, Donald Trump?" my mother says. "He's a big, fat take-it-yourself dunk."

In some Alzheimer's homes, they put a bus stop in front so that people wandering will simply sit and wait. And the moment cycles, again and again, until someone notices they are missing and they are found.

Pointing at Javi, you sometimes ask, "And where is her *mother*?"

Precious Lizzie,

Her nickname was Tempi.

Love, Mom

# All Knotted Up

DANA PRESCOTT

"Your father could make conversation with a brick wall," my mother said. She was hanging laundry in the backyard of our house in Cohasset, a sea-side town south of Boston. From where we stood, we could see the blue ribbon of the Atlantic stretching along the horizon line. My parents were fresh back from a cruise where Dad had made innumerable new friends while mother, wrapped in blankets on the deck, sank deep into a book.

My father, a Michigan farm boy who left home at the age of seventeen to join the Merchant Marine, was an optimistic, gregarious, and social man whose knowledge base was broader and more idiosyncratic than anyone I have ever met. Even in his eighties, he would pass the hallway mirror and pause for a moment, murmuring, "You handsome, handsome man." Dad knew Morse code, how to pack a cargo ship to keep it from listing, how to navigate by reading the stars. Mostly, Dad knew the world of business, sales, and rope. He knew about knots, and he was occasionally consulted by the Boston Police Department if any kind of rope was used in a crime. More than once, detectives in blue uniforms pulled up in their cruisers to the curb of our lawn, carrying rope in a plastic bag.

"That there?" my dad would say, fingering the evidence through the plastic. "That was made in Manila by a firm—let me think—well, they went out of business in '72. Beautiful rope. And the knot, oh the knot is ama-teur, done in a hurry, and the guy who tied it is probably left-handed." Or "This? This would be Rhode Island, old New England family factory. See the yellow thread in the middle of the twist? That's the tracer. Mandatory in large diameter cordage like this. Nylon. So, that would be, I would guess, from Pawtucket."

He loved hard work, making a deal, closing a sale. His wood-paneled basement "retirement" office was a whirlwind of activity as he drove a bargain, imported netting from Portugal, sent out faxes, made long-distance phone calls. "Honey," he said to me, "you have never seen netting so beautiful." He called old contacts to whom he sold bailer twine, lobster bands, and cordage until he was ninety. He never stopped working. In the last months of his life, confined to a nursing home, he passed out business cards and talked with the doctor about getting a larger room if the man next door would hurry up and die so that my father could set up a proper office.

"You see, honey, people will always need rope," he told each of his four daughters repeatedly and as if it were a revelation. "From wrapping packages to making a noose—" Here he stopped for dramatic effect. "Hell, they will always need rope."

Dad had a big voice, big ideas, a big heart, and an even bigger temper. He would give you the shirt off his back if he loved you, but if you crossed him, he slammed doors and drawers, bellowed in anger, never forgot, rarely forgave. He once smashed a favorite dinner plate (we called it the "Jesus plate") into pieces because we sisters were arguing over whose turn it was to use it, and another time told me in fury, "You're going to drive me to drink . . ." He did drink too, and sometimes too much. Once he ended up in a fight and had to dry out overnight in a Boston jail. If Dad and we daughters were at our summerhouse in Maine and he stumbled home after dinner with friends, the next day he'd say, "Now there's no reason for your mother to know what went on last night."

No stranger to belligerence, he would punish, jeer, get even, threaten, and steam. He constantly crossed people off his list. After he had argued with the local dry cleaner, he switched over to one that was miles out of his way.

My three sisters and I would lock our bedroom doors when he got angry, fearful of his wrath, and that just made him madder. "Fine! Lock your door! But when you least expect it, you're going to GET IT!" As a parent, though, Dad's anger never actually resulted in more than bluster. He didn't shine to being a disciplinarian, and we didn't shine to being disciplined.

Dad was fascinated by people, and he was fascinated by himself. A big storyteller, he loved parties, public speaking, being in front of crowds, and he was delighted to be seated at the head of a table where he could best hold forth. En route to our summerhouse, we would wait restlessly while he visited clients in lobster shacks perched on wharfs. He spent hours talking with fishermen, sometimes while we sweltered in a hot car. Talking with a local seaman usually meant having a drink, regardless of the time of day. Upon returning to his disgruntled family, he often reeked of beer and cigarette smoke.

Years later, when he visited me at my home in Italy, I translated for him while he talked at length with a man whose company was making a new kind of concrete out of trash. He learned, from another Italian craftsman, everything about how a pizza oven conducts heat. He knew that great teachers are seldom where you would expect them to be. Rarely behind a university desk, the scholars of the real world have no advanced degrees and are living and working within it.

As with many salesmen of his generation, my father's work meant extensive travel. His infrequent stops at home sometimes seemed like a cruel interruption into our daily routines. He also made us work. He had us girls splicing rope down in the basement for custom orders, fifty cents a splice.

A client once wanted cordage Dad had on hand but wanted it to be yellow rather than the standard white. Dad knew that particular kind of rope was not made in yellow, so he filled our bathtub with yellow dye, draped the dyed rope over a clothesline till dry, coiled it up, and met the delivery date. "Dad, won't it fade in the salt water?" I asked. "Of course!" he said. "But I held up my end of the deal. It's yellow rope when he gets it; what happens next is his problem."

Frankly, my mother was more fun when he was gone. We had "backward dinners" with dessert served first (usually fruit slices and cottage cheese, as my mom was an early health food / no sugar enthusiast), or we picnicked on the living room floor. She seemed more relaxed and would read to us longer before bedtime. Home, with Dad away, was my refuge, a buzz of books and plays and projects, dress-ups and hours of reading. I would enter the house from the breezeway, slam the door behind me, and yell out, "MOM, I'm HOME!" And best of all, our mother occasionally kept us home from school to "further our education."

"Dear Mr. Kraemer," I remember her writing as she said the words aloud. "Today is such a beautiful day"—pause for emphasis as she looked around the Formica table at our four expectant faces—"I will be keeping my girls home with me."

She took us to collect storm clams after hurricanes, to pick apples and blueberries. She pined for the New York City life and family she had left to follow my dad to New England, so many of these excursions were into Boston, to see exhibits at the Museum of Fine Arts or shop for bargains in the basement of Filene's department store. She loved being with us, we were the center of her life, and we, in turn, loved being with her. When I heard Dad's car tires crunch the gravel in the driveway, my heart sank. My father might be tipsy; he might be in a bad mood. He conducted his life and his marriage and family in a stubborn "I am the head of this family" manner. This did not sit well with me. I was in high school, it was the seventies, and I was a proud and budding feminist. I loved the sound of that word, *feminist*. I would lie on my bed and say, "That's what I am, I am a *feminist*," and I found my father's treatment of my mother to be out of touch and downright wrong. "Where's the salt?" he'd bellow from his seat at the table. Every time, Mom jumped to her feet and fetched the salt.

Our family rode not only the unpredictable waves of my father's moods but also the up-and-down economics of his profession as a salesman. We knew how sales things were going without asking him by whether we drank our orange juice full strength or watered down.

Dad's barreling voice never ceased to embarrass me, even well into my adulthood. In Umbria, Italy, where I work with artists from around the world, he once asked in a too-loud voice, as a photographer from New

York approached the lunch table, "Who's the blonde?" And another time, as a Korean friend discussed politics with him, he asked, "What do you Orientals think about our president?" No one seemed as bothered by this as I was. "It's generational," my mom would say in his defense. "He doesn't *intend* to offend . . ." We were to respect my father, to be grateful to him, to be good Christian children. My mother had been "saved" at a Billy Graham crusade shortly after marrying my father, and we were raised with Billy Graham principles at work.

As much as I found sustenance, laughter, and comfort in my childhood home, I, like my father, left young. I wonder often, if, like my father, I had wanderlust or if I was running away from something, or perhaps both. Along with the deep love I drank in under my parents' roof, I often felt the evangelical Christian doctrines to be suffocating. Bible stories gave me nightmares, I was afraid of the dark, afraid of the devil and evil spirits. People in our church, including my mom, spoke in tongues, were baptized as adults, were "slain by the spirit," or had healing powers. It all frightened me, I wanted to escape it, but mostly, I was curious about the rest of the world; I wanted to travel, I wanted to define who I was growing up to be. Perhaps like my father, the youngest of four boys, I, one of four girls, was anxious to shed my provincial past and make something of myself in a larger world. I left home in my twenties, and as the years unfolded, I moved thousands of miles away from family, married, and with my husband, raised our son in Italy. I shed the religious environment in which I had been raised, and on top of that, I married a Jewish man. We rarely darkened the door of a synagogue or church unless for a marriage or funeral.

I missed the hymn sings in our Baptist church, but I didn't miss all the rules and regulations. We weren't supposed to dance or drink or swear or date, all things I longed to do, all things that, after all, my father did or had done. In later years, I grew so grateful for my Baptist upbringing—it taught me all the essential stories I needed to understand Renaissance painting. I missed my family's table and food, but I didn't miss seeing Dad mix up another orange juice and vodka or slam his fist on the table making the cutlery leap into our laps.

As my own family life in Italy unfolded, I did what I did best: I painted, I wrote, I taught. My artistic life (thank you, Mother) was always balanced with practical concerns (thank you, Dad). "You can do what you want," my father said, "so long as you can pay your own taxes." So my nonlucrative painting-writing life was always supported by a professional job that paid the bills. I learned about administration, organizational behavior, and budgets while still showing work or publishing the occasional travel essay. I moved into academic administration, but I was well into my fifties before I landed what was to be the most meaningful work of my life, directing the Civitella Ranieri Foundation, an international arts residency housed in a fifteenth-century Umbrian castle.

A typical Civitella workday might begin with a walk around the property with Maurizio, the custodian and groundskeeper. We talk about when he plans to prune the roses, how to block the rain from coming through roof tiles, the strange horned beetles he has been finding in the cypress trees. I drop by the kitchen and the vegetable garden, occasionally lending a hand with making sauce if there is a huge bounty of tomatoes. I love to help harvest the lemons, the olives, the sweet-sour *fragolino* grapes that form an arbor at the music studio we call Pizza on account of its large outdoor oven.

I eat lunch with my fellows, ask about their work, their home nations, their families, and their goals. I visit a studio or read a manuscript draft. I finish up my office work, take a walk with the dog, introduce a visiting speaker, help field audience questions, raise a toast at dinner, and once it's over, pour digestifs into the elegantly mismatched collection of cordial glasses that lived for decades on my mother's sideboard. In many ways, Civitella is a family, it is my family, a safe harbor, for our international fellows who leave complicated lives behind for a few weeks to concentrate fully on their work. Building Civitella, nurturing Civitella, protecting Civitella, it is not so different from my childhood, sharing chores, defending my sisters, talking with whomever is seated next to you, finding common ground.

In hindsight, my escape from the intensity of my childhood and family life was not accidental. Before my son was born, I had been happy to shed the responsibilities that come with a close-knit family. I couldn't get far enough away. But with his birth, who I was and what I had inherited from my family became more important. I ended up far from home but in a familiar context, thanks to my mother's Northern Italian ancestry and her love of all things Italian. My father, too, revered her Italian-ness, confiding often to anyone who would listen, "I married my wife because her apartment smelled like tomato sauce."

The surprise outcome of my self-imposed exile from my childhood and family is that I now find myself professionally, personally, and geo-graphically in a place where success is based on everything I learned as a child from my dramatically different but equally influential mother and father. Because of my father, I love a good martini, the laughter and company of crowds, travel, working hard, and oddly enough, poetry, long stanzas of which he had committed to memory.

Because of my mother, I find solace in reading; I recharge through long periods of time alone; I have a profound love for beauty, be it in a landscape or a museum. Like my mother, I love to dance, to laugh ridic-ulously loudly; I take pride in a beautifully set table, the world of art and music, a well-tailored suit, and a shopping bargain.

Because of both my parents, having people gathered around the eve-ning dinner table is essential in my life. At Civitella, as I sit beneath the ivy-crowned pergola and the evening darkens like a blanket around us, the conversations with international colleagues become more frank and honest. In those moments, I realize my life has re-created my childhood dinner table, where conversation, laughter, lifelong connections, curiosity about the world, ideas, aspirations, and love were all born.

And as for rope, I can still tie a mean bowline and a half hitch, an eminently practical bit of know-how.

# Sisters

ANN PATCHETT

I was probably ten the first time a cashier in the grocery store asked my mother and me if we were sisters. At the time I thought that the cashier meant we resembled one another, and to some extent that was true. I was blond like my mother, with small shoulders and light eyes. My sister had brown hair and skin that tanned to gold just by walking out the door. People were much less likely to ask my mother and my sister if they were sisters, though surely that had to do with the fact that my sister was three and a half years older than I was and made it her personal mission to never be with us in the grocery store. (No one ever asked my sister and me if we were sisters, probably because we were sisters, and even though we didn't much resemble one another, the electrical current that ran between us was self-evident.) The question posed by the cashier was a compliment for me—my mother was beautiful—but mostly it was meant as a compliment for her: You look so young! How could you be the mother of this big girl?

My mother was twenty-six when I was born, and her twenties was the decade in which she took up indefinite residence. Her youthfulness was such that she was carded in bars late into her forties. Everyone got older but her. When I was in high school, I wore one of her nightgowns to the prom. She was out of town, and I didn't know it was a nightgown. As far as I was concerned, it was just another great dress hanging in her closet. (Note: my mother hung up her nightgowns.) Later, when I told my mother about the dress, and she told me what I'd done, my friends and I all laughed about it. Her nightgown trumped their prom dresses. My friends were all in love with my mother, with her zip-up boots and E-type Jaguar and her thick yellow ponytail. My mother would write notes for anyone who had spent the night at our house and was late for school the next morning. "She's more like a sister," my friends would say, not meaning that we looked like one another.

By the time I was in college, whatever resemblance we had shared before was harder to see—not exactly gone and not exactly obvious. My hair had faded to a color I liked to call "dead mouse" and I'd put on weight, two things that hadn't happened to my mother. I was a little taller than she was. I no longer fit into her clothes. I came home from school and the bank teller stared at us earnestly, as if she was coming upon someone she couldn't quite place. "Are you two sisters?" she asked. And that was what she meant: are the two of you the offspring of one set of parents?

My mother, who looked like a cross between a Hitchcock heroine and one of John Derek's wives, had drawn a winning ticket from the genetic lottery. Had she followed my example and done nothing more than wash her face and walk out the door in the morning, she would still have been the most beautiful woman you would see on any given day; but my mother left nothing to chance. She skipped desserts and dinner rolls, was fully committed to moisturizer and sunscreen. She had a collection of silk underwear—tap pants and camisoles, teddies, chemises in every color—and when she changed her clothes, she started at the beginning and changed her lingerie as well, the things that no one would see, because the lingerie was all part of it. The best hours of my childhood were spent sitting on the edge of the bathtub watching her put on her makeup and roll her hair. The bag boys in the grocery store argued as to who would push her cart out to her car, and once or twice the winner tried to kiss her. She had to have checks printed without her phone number because the man in the liquor store would call and ask her on dates. Was gorgeousness such a rarity in those days? In restaurants someone would inevitably come to the table to tell us, just in case we didn't know, that my mother was a vision—the most beautiful woman he or she had ever seen. My mother would thank the person while the rest of us just kept eating.

I grew up, grew older. I didn't color my hair or buy mascara. I aspired to a look that was clean, well-kempt, invisible; and in this I was successful. I had seen the benefits and costs of beauty and decided to pass. A lucky call on my part, since even though I was nice enough looking, I possessed neither the raw material nor the willingness to try and improve the hand I'd been dealt. I like to think my mother's beauty saved me time, by which I mean years and years of my life. Despite all indications to the contrary, most women harbor some secret hope that they might be beautiful, that the right dress or lipstick or diet could turn the tide in their favor. As someone who had lived with exceptional beauty, I harbored no such illusions.

It's important for people to believe that beautiful women are narcissists, and that they've been punished for what they've unfairly received. While she was certainly punished for her beauty by jealous husbands and jealous friends, and by her older sister who liked to announce to anyone who would listen that my mother got the looks but she—the sister—had gotten all the brains, my mother was never a narcissist. She worked as a nurse for most of her life. She possessed an uncanny knack for comforting people, for knowing the right thing to say and knowing when to say nothing at all. Men liked her best, but so did dogs and children. She was funny and kind and, no matter what her sister would tell you, smart. She was also beautiful.

As I went through my thirties and forties, my sisterhood with my mother became a given. The questions were no longer questions, they were statements of fact. When someone said, "Sisters, right?" I said, "You got it." In fact, I was starting to be the older sister. I could imagine a time when I would be the mother.

If my mother was the one who answered the question, she always told the truth. She was the progenitor after all—she was proud of me. Once, when I was in my forties, we stopped by my publishing house in New York to drop off some papers. The security guard at the desk took our IDs. "You two sisters?" he asked suspiciously.

"She's my daughter," my mother said.

The man handed us back our driver's licenses and looked at me. "What are you doing wrong?"

I laughed. "You're supposed to ask her what she's doing right."

"I know what I said." His tone was flat, accusatory. "I said, what are you doing wrong?"

Every now and then I did it right, and that's when trained professionals were paid to do it for me. When I was on television or had my picture taken for a magazine, other people dressed me in clothes that weren't mine and then someone else straightened, curled, and sprayed my hair while a third person painted an entirely new face on top of my face. Then even I must admit I looked something like my mother. Sometimes I went to see my mother after I had been photographed as an author. Sometimes we went out to lunch before I could get hold of a washcloth and scrub my face. The twenty-six years my mother had on me could almost balance out the inequality, assuming we were both wearing a layer of makeup. The waitress put her hand to her heart. "Seriously?" she said. "Are you two twins?"

"Sisters," I said.

There was one other time we came close to evening out, and that's when my mother was sick. It happened three years ago, before she turned eighty. She had such a terrible pain beneath her lower ribs that I drove her to the hospital in a rainstorm, in the middle of the night. There was no time for makeup, no time to pack. The doctor in the emergency room sent her straight to the intensive care unit, and we stayed there for a week. She slept in a bed inside a glass room, and I slept in a chair beside her. She had a walled-off infection in her upper duodenum. She sweated through her nightgown and sheets and then shook so hard I would climb into her bed and hold her. Doctors and nurses and phlebotomists and the housekeeping staff moved through her fish bowl room every fifteen minutes to check on one thing or another, and there they observed the two pale women in a single bed who didn't eat or sleep or wash but who laid there together, arms around waists like a mother and daughter in bed beneath the scorching florescent lights. It would be safe to say we had never looked worse.

"You look so much alike," the nurse would say quietly, not wanting to disturb us more than we were already disturbed.

"Like sisters?" I asked.

She shook her head. "No," she said, "like the same person."

# One Man's Poison

Before my mother's suicide the year I turned twelve, my father and I seldom saw each other. An engineer who became a board director at a steel-manufacturing conglomerate, Hiroshi traveled all over the country on business. Even when he worked in his office in Kobe, he left early and came back—if he came back—past midnight. My mother waited up, but he often called from some noisy bar to claim he was leaving on a business trip. Other phone calls, from women looking for him, made clear that my father had several girlfriends who vied for his attention. I can't remember a time when I didn't know that he was a liar and a cheat and that women were attracted to him all the same.

Since his free time was devoted to playing rugby with former college teammates, Hiroshi seldom joined my mother, brother, and me on family vacations or outings. He did once attend a family reunion—for his side of the family—at a Chinese restaurant in downtown Kobe. My brother, Jumpei, four years younger than I, was still a toddler. When we got to the restaurant, our relatives hadn't arrived yet, the banquet room wasn't ready, and my mother had to take Jumpei to the bathroom. I was left to sit at the bar with Hiroshi while we waited. He must have had to help me up to the barstool, but I don't remember him lifting me or holding me on that occasion or any other. What I do recall is the woman behind the bar placing a glass of soda pop in front of me, smiling in an exaggerated way, and saying, "You look just like your father. How lucky for you. He is so very handsome."

Even though the woman's face was just a few inches from mine, her eyes were turned to my father. She was young enough that, a few minutes later while recounting this incident to my mother in the bathroom—where she had to take me to wash the tears from my face, bringing my brother back with us too—I would refer to the woman as *oneisan* (big sister, or young woman) rather than *obasan* (auntie, or middle-aged woman). "That *oneisan* was wrong. I don't look anything like him," I insisted. When my mother suggested maybe I did just a little, I started crying again.

I always knew that my father failed to treat my mother with love or respect, but he wasn't home often or long enough to care what I said or did until a few weeks after her death, when one of his girlfriends moved into our house. He had met Michiko at the business hotel her parents managed, where he was a frequent guest. Once they were married, a couple of months later, he started cheating on her too. Michiko couldn't help what Hiroshi did away from home, but unlike my mother, she knew how to get his attention. Whenever he started staying out too much, she told him that I had made her so miserable by disrespecting her in his absence that she wanted to leave us. She sat with her suitcase packed while he beat me in front of her and made me apologize. For a few weeks after, he came home earlier than usual and spent his weekends watching TV with her instead of playing rugby. But soon enough, he would be back to his old ways, till one night, he'd find her waiting in the kitchen with her packed suitcase.

I left home at twenty to attend college in Illinois, settled in Wisconsin to go to graduate school and teach creative writing at a small college, and only saw my father three times after—once in New York when he and Michiko were on a tour with his rugby group, twice in Japan when I was visiting relatives on my mother's side. Each visit lasted just long enough to get through a meal at a restaurant. He complained that New York was dirty and full of homeless people. He said he was saddened by my getting a PhD in English because I should have studied the literature of our country first. When he died from cancer, I was thirty-seven and married, living and teaching in Green Bay. In Japan, cancer patients are kept in the dark about their prognosis, though he must have sensed how sick he was. My stepmother, who had been fully informed by the doctors, didn't contact me—seeing me would only upset him, she reasoned. Michiko needn't have worried. I wouldn't have gone to say goodbye even if Hiroshi himself had asked me to.

During my father's life, it never occurred to me that I was anything like him. I'm not a habitual liar or a sexual adventurer (or whatever the female or gender-neutral equivalent of "womanizer" is). The lies I tell are relatively harmless, like claiming to be working on a project I promised and forgot about (then starting it right away). I found it too exhausting to maintain a romantic relationship with one person at a time. I can't imagine carrying on with half a dozen lovers the way Hiroshi did. I'm now divorced and happily single. I chose not to have children so I never had to worry about becoming a terrible parent like my father, who teetered between neglect and domination, indifference and rage.

Even though I was the only person in our family whom Hiroshi had yelled at and hit, I don't think he did these things only to appease Michiko. He was truly angry and out of control on the nights he beat me. He considered me (rather than his own behavior) as a threat to his second marriage, and the thought of losing the stability and the convenience he had reestablished after my mother's suicide enraged him. I have never yelled at anyone in anger, much less physically assaulted them. The worst things my husband and I said to each other in the fifteen years we were married were (him) "You might be the most selfish person I've ever met" and (me) "That includes your mother?" Twenty years after our divorce, we're still friends and we periodically apologize to each other for these remarks.

Still, it's not difficult to be patient and reasonable with adults—they can be patient and reasonable to you in return or else you can politely walk away. Whenever I come across small children screaming and running around the grocery store or having temper tantrums in a park, something inside me winces and clenches. I wonder what keeps their parents from covering their ears and banging their own heads against the wall or getting in the car and driving away alone. Perhaps my father felt the same way around children, but remaining childless wasn't an acceptable option for married couples of my parents' generation. That doesn't excuse how he neglected me through my childhood, only to beat me for the eight years I had to live with him and his second wife. He could at least have tried to moderate his extreme reactions. He had no conscience whatsoever. I didn't fear becoming Hiroshi because he was beyond the pale, in a category by himself.

So I believed it was my mother, not my father, whose legacy required careful navigation. I wanted to be like her in all the right ways while avoiding the one wrong way that had led to her death. Takako was a creator of beauty. She sketched and drew, told stories and wrote amusing letters that her parents kept to pass on to me. She coaxed roses to twine around our garden gate, irises to bloom in our rock garden, and hydrangeas to turn pink, blue, or any shade in between. My friends envied the dresses she sewed for me, the blouses she embroidered, the cakes she baked and decorated for my birthday parties. All the women in the neighborhood gathered at our house to drink tea, work on their sewing and embroidery projects, and try out new recipes. "Your mother brought people together," one of them told me after her death. "She lit up the room just by walking in."

But after our family moved to a new neighborhood, Takako lost the energy to do anything. Every day for the next two years while my brother and I were at school, she sat alone in the kitchen, which faced north and was cold and dark, going over what she believed were her failures. Writing in her diary was about the only thing she still managed to do. She must have been angry at Hiroshi's betrayal, but in all the pages she filled in the red notebook she would leave behind, she didn't ask, "What is wrong with my husband?" or even "Why was I stupid enough to marry a man like this?" The question she asked repeatedly was, "What's wrong with me?" She couldn't get away from the thoughts that went around and around in her head: she was a failure as a wife and a mother, her whole life was worthless and meaningless, and we would all be better off without her. She didn't call her friends, sisters, brothers, or parents for help. She couldn't even make herself get up from the kitchen table and move to a more comfortable or cheerful part of the house. All the things she couldn't do to help herself made her feel even worse.

Although my mother was never officially diagnosed—the idea of seeking a medical intervention added to her feelings of failure and shame—it's clear that she suffered from some form of depression. Other women of her generation, including the poets Sylvia Plath and Anne Sexton, had also killed themselves, leaving behind their children. As a young woman studying to be a writer in the decades after their deaths, I feared that someday I might find myself sitting in a dark kitchen going over all the ways in which I had wasted my life and become a failure. I didn't think any of these women had been killed by their writing, but the introspection required to compose poems—or diary entries in my mother's case—was difficult and dangerous work. You couldn't write anything true, complex, or beautiful unless you were willing to examine the unsettling thoughts in your own head; you had to force yourself to contemplate the random nature of the world and the limitations of human goodness. Getting depressed might be an occupational hazard. I wondered how I could be like these smart, creative women—my actual mother and my literary mothers—without inheriting their fate.

The last day I was forty-one, the age my mother had killed herself, I was in Cambridge, Massachusetts, signing the papers to purchase a studio apartment on the top floor of a condominium. I had left my marriage because I was at my happiest alone; I was moving to the East Coast for a new teaching job. The first home that was entirely mine, that studio was more like a nest than a piece of real estate. Sitting at my desk by the window overlooking the tops of maples, I felt solid contentment, the opposite of the bewildering displacement my mother had experienced after our family's move. There wasn't an aha moment when I realized that I was as immune to depression as a person could be, but I know the death of my father, six years prior, and the move east had combined to produce this understanding. I was no longer living in the first place—the American Midwest—where I'd settled to get away from him.

The lady bartender at the Chinese restaurant had been right. I did look like my father, though he was very handsome—people often said he resembled the actor Toshio Mifune, a rugged manly type who starred in several Kurosawa films—and I was only average looking. Sometimes when I glanced in the bathroom mirror in my new apartment, I recognized Hiroshi's eyes and mouth, the oval face with the pointed chin. My mother had been petite but womanly, with a round face and a slightly plump figure. I belonged unmistakably to my father's family, skinny and muscular, beginning to look a little gaunt in middle age while other women worried about putting on weight. Like my father, I was an aging athlete. A lot of my free time went to long-distance running and cycling, as his did to rugby. We were both too physically restless to sit around feeling bad about ourselves.

Now that he was safely gone and I was twice removed from my childhood in Japan, I could admit I was more like him than I ever was like my mother. When things didn't go my way, whether it was a disagreement with a neighbor or a rejection by a publisher, the first question on my mind was not, "What is wrong with me?" My immediate response, like Hiroshi's, was to blame someone or something else. I didn't raise my voice in anger, but my conviction that *I* was right was ironclad, no less so than my father's. I had learned to back off from this initial position of self-righteousness to consider the other person's view, to compromise or even be persuaded all the way to the other side, but that's more about the power of education than about my essential nature.

Unlike my mother, I didn't think someone lying to me or treating me with disrespect was my fault. Nor was I given to doubting and second-guessing myself once I had made an important decision I couldn't take back. As soon as our family had settled into our new house, my mother had started feeling that we should never have moved. She missed her friends, our old neighborhood, our old home. She even thought, for a while, that we could sell the new house and move back to the old one—and when it was too late for that, she talked about finding another house in the old neighborhood. I'm sure she knew that none of this was practical, or really possible. But once she started thinking about the outcome, she could no longer reverse—the decisions she had made and couldn't unmake—she couldn't stop trying to figure out what had gone wrong. She sat for hours in that house she hated, in the neighborhood where she knew no one, reexamining the now-useless details over and over. Ultimately, she was killed by the persistence of her thoughts.

My father, on the other hand, made his decisions, good or bad, large or small, and moved on. In the first week after my mother's death, her youngest brother, Kenichi—who was single and childless—stayed at our house to look after my brother and me while Hiroshi went back to work. On the nights Kenichi was still up when Hiroshi returned, the two men had a few drinks together. "Your father cried when he drank whiskey," Kenichi told me years later. "He said your mother was a remarkable woman. He didn't deserve her. He even said, 'You know I killed her.' He cried big, big tears." Two weeks later, Hiroshi would tell Kenichi he was no longer needed at our house. "The woman I'm going to marry is moving here this weekend," he said to my uncle. "She doesn't have children of her own. She's agreed to raise mine."

Once he was with Michiko, Hiroshi never mentioned Takako except to make me cry on those nights he hit me in front of his new wife. "Your mother didn't love you enough to stick around," he said. "She left you to be a burden to me." Other than those remarks, it was as though Takako had never even existed. He no longer spoke or wrote to his former in-laws and kept my brother and me from seeing them till we were adults.

Hiroshi succeeded in erasing Takako from my brother's memory. The few times I saw him after I left home, Jumpei referred to Michiko as "my mother" rather than "my stepmother." He claimed he had no recollection of Takako. "I was too young," he said. "I only have one mother, the one who raised me." At our mother's death, he had been eight, which strikes me as too old for total amnesia—I remember plenty of things from when I was four or five, maybe even three—but my brother is devoted to Michiko. He was the one to call me with the news of Hiroshi's death. He asked me to come to Japan, though I would not arrive in time for the funeral. The real purpose of the visit, as it turned out, was for me to sign the numerous legal documents required to designate Michiko as the sole heir to Hiroshi's estate.

In Japan, few people leave wills. By law, 50 percent of a dead man's estate goes to his spouse, with the other 50 percent to be divided equally among the children, but most families with significant wealth choose just one person—either the wife or the oldest son—to inherit it all. My brother had never lived in his own apartment, married, or held a regular job. For decades, he had been operating an import-export business of South American folk art—a venture kept afloat by our family's money. He spent most of the year traveling abroad, and for the few months he was in Japan, he stayed with Hiroshi and Michiko. My father left enough money for all of us to live with some comfort. If I signed what was somewhat ominously referred to as the "renunciation documents," Michiko would claim all the assets but continue to support her "son," and eventually, my brother would inherit whatever was left. I took the envelope Michiko gave me back to the hotel room where I was staying. I sat down on the bed, opened the envelope, and signed the whole stack of papers. I didn't comply to help my family. The executed documents were my ticket to freedom. I would never have to hear from Michiko or Jumpei once I handed them over. Twenty years later, it's as though I no longer exist for them, or they for me.

I am my father's daughter in this way. Once I commit to a course of action, I don't look back with longing at what's been lost as a result or contemplate how things might have been different. This faith in the future we chose is a form of arrogance. It assumes that any important decision we made has to be the right one because, after all, we made it. The difference between us is that when I do change my mind, I'm willing to admit that I had been really, truly wrong. My father went from one self-serving reality to another, each time convinced that his interpretation or his view was right in a new way. He was able to carry on affairs with several women while being married to my mother by believing that in every moment, he was being true to his precious self. He could cry big tears about my mother one week and plan Michiko's move into our house the next because to him everything he felt and thought was equally true and important. Just like that, he could go from confiding in my uncle to asking him to leave. With perfect consistency, Hiroshi did what was right for himself; he had no regrets.

My father was a complete narcissist. The pragmatic selfish streak he passed on to me is undoubtedly a poison. But in small doses, it can be a form of medicine, like a weakened virus that immunizes us against life-threatening illness. My mother's legacy, too, is a potent substance that can sustain me or kill me. Her tendency to brood, to ask too many questions, to stay with the same thoughts all day long, fuels my writing. On the page, I can examine the endless layers of possibilities and interpretations, how things could, might, should have been, why they weren't, and what that means. I dive into the murky depths of my own thoughts to examine the unsettling ideas lurking there, but I'm not easily overwhelmed by what I find. I reserve this kind of rigorous contemplation for my writing: I don't torment myself by questioning and examining every detail of my life in real time. I refuse to be crippled by self-doubt and regret. My father's poison allows me to move through a world full of betrayals and failures without taking everything to heart. In fact, I inherited the right amount to immunize myself from the greatest danger of all: my father himself.

If I had been more like my mother, I would have been destroyed by all the nights he dragged me into the kitchen to apologize to Michiko, the numerous belittling comments he tossed my way even after I put an ocean between us. When Hiroshi blamed me for Michiko's unhappiness, I knew that the real reasons for the packed suitcase were the lies he told her and the nights he failed to come home. It wasn't my fault that Michiko had knowingly married a man who cheated on his wife and continued to do the same. It never occurred to me that Hiroshi attacked me instead of protecting me because something was wrong with me. I didn't agonize over why he didn't love me or what I could do to change this fact. A few years before he died, I had stopped responding to the letters he wrote criticizing my modest teaching job "out in the middle of nowhere" and berating my failure to "learn first about your own culture." The only way not to be hurt by him was to erase him from my life, the way he had erased my mother from his. I survived being his daughter by acting just like he did.

# Unlived Lives

One afternoon in the early 1990s, my mother and grandmother sat down in my kitchen. This, I felt then and know now, was a momentous, unprecedented, and as it turned out, unrepeated occasion. My whole adult life, up until that day, I had been the guest, returning for the occasional holiday to the Southern California ranch house where I grew up or visiting the apartment in a Boston suburb where my grandmother lived alone in the long decades after my grandfather's death. I'd spent so much time underfoot, rummaging their cupboards, searching for the dessert plates or a slotted spoon—is there any quicker way to feel superfluous than in another woman's kitchen? My own place was a San Francisco studio I doted upon even though the drunks who tumbled out of the dive bar across the street in the wee hours made for some noisy nights. Now my mom and her mother were on my turf.

I liked to believe that even when I was on *their* turf, I carried a capsule of insurrection inside me, like a spy's microfilm. My grandmother and my mother had married young and focused on being housewives and mothers. I've never married, and that studio apartment marked the beginning of a long love affair with living alone. My grandmother would show me photos of my cousins' kids and tell me how much I was missing. My mother would pester me about adopting a more conventionally feminine look. I assured my grandmother that I had no doubts about forgoing motherhood and insisted, obnoxiously, on wearing a Ramones t-shirt in a series of professional photos my parents had taken of our family. I chose to live in a city rather than the suburbs. My friends were performance artists and sex advice columnists and opera singers. Instead of driving a station wagon, I rode around town on a Vespa with roses painted all over it. I remembered well my mother explaining to my child self that writing wasn't a job you could make a living at, but on the afternoon she sat at my vintage yellow Formica table, I was nearly to the point where I could.

There's an old joke that the quickest and easiest way to make a woman angry is to tell her how much she resembles her mother. I am far from the first daughter to purposely set out to live a life entirely different from her mom's. Of course, it never occurred to me that my own mother probably thought she'd done the same thing. The daughter of a foreman at a razor blade factory, she'd married a man who was non-Catholic, an MIT graduate, and an intellectual; then they'd moved all the way across the country to live in a neighborhood where half the land was still covered in chaparral and the raw diggings of new construction. Their friends wore capris, campaigned for JFK, and sat cross-legged on the floor drinking red wine out of plastic cups and listening to folk music. My mother married in the 1950s, raised five kids in the 1960s, and by the time the '70s showed up to turn tradition and expectation on their heads, she was ready. Around that time, I discovered a plastic margarine tub full of seedy marijuana in my parents' bedroom. Well indoctrinated by my public school's antidrug programs, I was horrified and surreptitiously flushed it down the toilet.

The women on my mother's side of the family do not mince words. When I ushered my mother and her mother into my beloved studio, I was surely bracing myself to be nitpicked. The apartment would be too small, the intersection too noisy, and didn't I want a husband and a house of my own? Instead, my mother looked around a bit, then turned to my grandmother and said, "You know, I would have loved to live in a cute little place like this after I got out of school and before I married Jim." This astonished me, but not as much as my grandmother's next remark, "You mean, when you worked at the radio station?"

I'd always understood my mother to have followed a sedate, preordained path from girlhood to marriage. She attended the sort of all-girls Catholic school where the nuns freaked out whenever a man set foot on campus; then she earned a nursing degree from Boston College. She went out at night in Dior New Look–style gowns with tight, pink satin bodices and clouds of tulle skirts to dances where she filled out actual dance cards with the names of undergraduate boys dressed in formal jackets. I found a handful of these cards when my siblings and I were cleaning out the house after her death a few years ago, along with a photo of her at about age nineteen laughing giddily into the camera with a camellia corsage on her wrist. If a nice Catholic girl were going to work, then nursing was just the sort of job she should pursue; it would throw her into the company of eligible young doctors. (As it was, my dad, soon to be an aerospace engineer, beat the doctors to it.)

Working at a radio station, on the other hand, was not the right sort of work, and this was the first I'd ever heard of my mother doing it. Radio stations were the habitat of dicey characters like journalists, advertising salesmen, and worst of all, musicians. As I listened to my mother and grandmother reminisce about this job—a summer job, it seemed, a bit like an internship—Mom sounded wistful, longing, in a way she almost never did except when talking about her adored Uncle Nick, who was run over by a streetcar when she was twelve.

"I wanted to get a real job there," she said. "It seemed so exciting, being a journalist."

"Why didn't you?" I asked.

"Oh," she sighed, "there was no way for a woman to get ahead in that business. I would have just been a secretary." Nursing offered better pay, she said, and also more authority.

After each of my parents' deaths, a friend or two would pull me aside at the wake or take me out to dinner and unload a raft of memories. The stories they told me about Mom and Dad proved enlightening but also often perplexing. My father, constantly scolded by my mother for his detached approach to parenting, had devoted hours to tutoring or counseling adult friends who'd gone back to school or decided, as he had, when he became an attorney, to attempt a career change. They praised his generosity with his time and his patience. "It's so strange hearing these stories about how he helped all these people," one of my sisters remarked. "We didn't see that side of him at home." Our mothers and fathers can be the most familiar people in the world and total strangers; they have a dark side, like the moon, that's invisible to us as long as we remain locked in the fixed orbit of the parent-child bond. After both my parents had died, their friends told me things about them I'd never known, but it was my mother's own revelation in my kitchen that changed my image of her, and myself, the most dramatically.

"Nothing has a stronger influence psychologically . . . on their children than the unlived life of the parent," Carl Jung wrote. Stage mothers, or fathers who push their sons into athletics and then take the competition with other kids' teams far too seriously, are usually seen as archetypal examples of this principle. They make the vicarious nature of their ambitions for their kids all too obvious. But I'd had no clue during my fledgling years as a journalist that my mother had once contemplated doing—had actually *yearned* to do—more or less the same thing.

Likewise, it was news to me that she'd ever wanted to live alone. She had been an indefatigable nagger on the subject of family dinners, trips, and other rituals of togetherness. "Why can't you be more like the Waltons?" she wailed at her children whenever we wheeled off in pursuit of our individual projects and interests. She loved the way that TV clan of poor Virginia farmers during the Great Depression would call goodnight to each other at the end of every episode, while through their big, rambling house the lights winked out one by one. Her favorite books as a girl, she often informed us, were the *Happy Hollisters* series, about a family that solves mysteries together. She implied more than once that she'd wanted to have five children because that's how many the Hollisters had. We rolled our eyes, groaned, then ran off to follow our kid imperatives; her vision of domestic intimacy seemed the opposite of adventure.

I can't remember the rest of my mother's and grandmother's visit to my San Francisco apartment. There's a strong possibility I would have forgotten it entirely if that conversation hadn't flipped my understanding of myself in relation to my mom. Up until that point, I'd wanted to believe that I had shrugged off my upbringing, rejected my mother's and grandmother's choices and embarked on a course that they could barely comprehend (although I did want them to be impressed by it). I hadn't reckoned with the possibility that my mother might harbor her own rebellious impulses, let alone that she might, by some mysterious form of osmosis, have transmitted them to me. In trying to defy her, I had ended up realizing many of her secret dreams. This is another way that parents resemble the moon: they exert invisible forces that shift the tides in our selves.

I wish I could say that I now grasp the extent and power of those forces, but the truth is I still don't entirely understand my mother. She was a difficult, unreflective, and often dishonest person who bristled at any attempt to delve into her inner life. I never felt close to her, not that I can remember. Every so often I learn something new, and it seems like a piece from an entirely different jigsaw puzzle. I remember that moment in my kitchen—when I first heard about this radio station job, about my mother's unmet wish to live on her own—as the point where I learned something small about her, and something much bigger about myself, the most important thing, really, that anyone can know, which is just how little they know.

# A Measure of Perversity

MARC MEWSHAW

When I was still a babe in arms, my father, a writer, shipped our family of four to Rome, Italy, in search of stimulation and respite from the sharp-elbowed American hustle. My family lived, frugally but comfortably, off the proceeds of my father's output, and thus his work had a centrality in our well-being (and our apartment) that can't be overstated. During office hours, generally between noon and seven, my brother and I were under orders to speak in whispers, pad around, ninja-like, in socks, and watch afterschool cartoons at a volume that turned us into master lip-readers.

Workaholic though he was behind closed doors, my father emerged from the cocoon of his toils a social butterfly, a great wit, a world-class raconteur, the funniest man at any given gathering. He'd always had a knack for winning friends, and he swanned about the ancient cobbles of Rome among the expat literary royalty: Gore Vidal, Pat Conroy, Graham Greene. It was in the lee of this towering presence, this man about town who churned out a novel a year, that I would eventually attempt to scratch out my own identity as a writer. His was a hard act to follow—one that I followed, blind drunk, through an Oedipal minefield.

But I'm getting ahead of myself.

For all my juvenile worship of my father, for all my attempts to turn myself into a carbon copy of him, there was one trait of his that never sat comfortably with me: what I'll call his perversity. Put simply, Mike Mewshaw is no joiner. To an extent many would find unseemly, upsetting, or simply odd, he has always run against the grain of social expectation. Out of distaste for the logistical and philosophical baggage of home ownership, he and my mother have never bought property. As far back as I can remember, he slept in till 10:30 or 11, appearances be damned. Even his decision to expatriate illustrates the large point: lighting out for Italy entailed giving up tenure as the head of the Creative Writing Department at the University of Texas; in other words, trading security and familiarity for hand-to-mouth precarity in a country that made a fetish of inconvenience and where we were never more than one false step away from deportation. But this was the price of a life less banal, and I think he thrilled to the notion of charting a course most middle-class Americans of the era saw as perplexingly unorthodox if not completely irrational.

In person, my father's nonconformism comes across as a tightly coiled energy, a prickly irreverence. He's nobody's fool, nor does he suffer them. And yet, for all his flashes of flippancy, he's blessed with a witty, anarchic charm. He has a genius for saying the unsayable and thereby taking the air out of the stodgy rituals of politesse. At cocktail parties swarming with stiffs, he'll often introduce himself as "Michael Mewshaw, gynecologist to the stars." Such acts of social sabotage serve a certain notice: whether you think me crazy or odd, your approval carries no weight; I play by different rules.

At bottom, I think his devilry springs from an allergy to triteness, to groupthink—an aversion rooted in his sense of what artistic originality demands: holding yourself defiantly, even aggressively aloof from prevailing worldviews and ideologies, the better to come at life from your own idiosyncratic slant. Just to get a rise out of *bien-pensants*, he's been known to launch into eye-wateringly off-color diatribes and adopt audaciously contrarian positions. For instance, he's never voted, and he's all too happy to share his rationale for his abstention. This particular set piece of his, while always good for a laugh, rarely fails to shock his listeners into fits of pique. Which, of course, is the whole point.

A further illustration of his drive to *épater la bourgeoisie*: his first ever reading was a scene in his debut novel, *Man in Motion*, of a woman shaving her privates. It was 1970, and he left the auditorium thunderstruck. Unbeknownst to him, several nuns were in attendance, one of whom pulled him aside at Mass the next day to deliver her diagnosis: you're a very sick young man.

But wait a moment. My father at Mass? The arch provocateur a practicing Catholic? How could this be? Simple. As I've heard him tell it, his faith solidified in the countercultural ferment of the sixties, when churchgoing was an act of intragenerational heresy.

The flipside of my father's iconoclasm is an unstinting fidelity to the truth. For him, this is as much an aesthetic as a personal crusade. He's forever in search of the grittier, more nuanced reality that Vaseline-lensed clichés, of thinking as of art, distort.

Nowhere is his contempt for cant and empty sentimentality more evident than in his career—and nowhere has it been more of a mixed blessing. In nonfiction, his specialty is the indignant exposé. Among other things, his investigations uncovered widespread corruption and sexual assault in the gentlemen's club known as the professional tennis circuit, the hypocrisies of the American penal code, the dark side of famous, widely beloved writers whose genius was shadowed by a monstrousness fawning that biographers and devotees tended to airbrush out of the picture.

I think my father would argue—and, here, I agree—that excavating the rot behind the whitewash is a public service. The trouble with skewering conventional wisdom and pulling heroes off their pedestals is that it doesn't always endear you to your readers. Most people want to smell the roses without their faces being rubbed in the fertilizer. And indeed, his tendency to go in for the takedown rather than the crowd-pleaser—in short, picking apart illusions rather than soothingly reaffirming them—has opened him up to charges of sour grapes, score-settling, and an unwholesome attraction to sordidness. He's faced career-threatening blowback, from a spell of pariahdom on the tennis tour, to wrenching betrayals by risk-averse publishers, to a libel suit (he was cleared, at great expense), to strained relations with communities of fellow writers.

At times, I've felt exasperated by his self-infliction of persona non grata status. Couldn't he see, I wondered in my teens and twenties, the link between his combativeness toward the establishment and the bruising he's often suffered at the hands of its gatekeepers? Did he have a blind spot around this? Or did he want it both ways—to rend people's safety blankets and simultaneously be loved for it?

Or was it something else? Did his need to prove himself more clear-sighted and unafraid of home truths than the blinkered masses trump everything else, including any consideration of how his outspokenness reflected on him or his family?

Congenital misfits that we are, my father and I couldn't be more alike. And yet, the differences are legion. Where my father is a pugnacious ruffler of feathers and stirrer of pots, I was—and to an extent, remain—a retiring people pleaser. As a kid, I strove for inconspicuousness, shrinking from conflict and controversy, swallowing my dissenting opinions, humoring the wrongheaded. Self-effacing to a fault, I went out of my way to defuse any threat I may have posed to others' self-regard or way of thinking. In short, if my father was always a little too heedless of appearances, I always cared a little too much.

That said, low-profile inoffensiveness was a survival strategy drilled into me by my gypsy upbringing, which, if nothing else, was an apprenticeship in imposture. We left Italy when I was ten, lived for five years in Charlottesville, Virginia, and moved to London for my high school years. Starting over again and again conditioned me to see myself from the point of view of outsiders and mold my personality, putty-like, around theirs. Though contexts and countries changed, the cardinal rules of shape-shifting never did: don't call attention to what makes you different; blend in or die. The downside of having become an astute mimic was living in perpetual anxiety of the slip that would out me as a fake.

Then too, in adolescence I began to feel squeamish about my father's rants and diatribes. I realized he wasn't always aware of the effect his unfiltered-ness had on others—or didn't care. Maybe in a bid to counterbalance him, then, I cultivated qualities that would cast me as the quiet, unassuming straight man to his unapologetically loud-mouthed jester.

And yet, all along, I felt vaguely ashamed of my conflict-avoidant ways. I knew I wanted to write, and insofar as my yardstick for writerdom was my father—bounding, strong-willed, gleefully transgressive—I felt my diffidence boded ill for my future as a man of letters. Where would I get my material if I was too hung up on how I was coming across to sally forth into the world? Still, it seemed only a matter of time before I blossomed into the dauntless figure I felt it was my birthright to become.

Puberty came and went, I learned how to drive, I turned eighteen—and still I waited to outgrow my larval meekness, increasingly alarmed that the long-awaited coming into my own might never materialize.

My first weekend at college, I got blackout drunk, face-planted on a curb, and woke up with sixteen stitches in my forehead. I didn't touch a drop of alcohol for another year.

By eerie happenstance, that same night, a kid in my dorm also got blackout drunk, face-planted on a curb, and knocked out his front teeth. This mishap had little effect on his alcohol intake.

When I drank next, it was with this young man, by then a full-fledged frat brother, when we traveled to Rome together over winter holidays the following year and stayed with my parents. I had my first-ever serious girlfriend, and the brotherhood of excess I was initiated into over the course of the ensuing weeklong bender felt of a piece with a larger trend toward maturity and adventure, a sloughing off of childhood's caution. We went clubbing, picked up girls, got into fistfights—this was living! One morning, my father woke to find me passed out in the bathroom, hugging the base of the toilet. The dressing down that followed was awful. Finding me prostrate and apparently dead, he told me, flashed him back to the terror as a child of coming across his stepfather in various states of inebriated collapse. He wasn't about to endure that harrowing trauma all over again—not under his own roof. He raged on, but what I remember most was the heartless smirk that broke over my face. The balance of power between us, I understood, had shifted: at last I had a lever over the old man. I returned to school a committed hard drinker. Within a year I was getting blackout drunk every night.

Why, I've often wondered, did booze and I get along so (in)famously when my father's drinking was always fairly temperate? I suppose it freed me from the worrywart circumspection that had tyrannized me since childhood, that tightly strung complex of rejection anxieties that had put a damper on my own peculiarities and skewed sense of humor lest I stick out and be ostracized. Drunk, I felt at last like the subversive showman in me—the one I'd been waiting for—was loosed from its hobbles. More to the point, I felt like a worthy heir to the Mewshaw mantle. I, too, could hold an audience in the palm of my hand, befriend people of all stripes, be the life of the party. I was, I thought, an optimized version of myself: swaggering, manically gregarious, quick-witted. Someone who got noticed.

Attachment to the frenzied ebullience booze released in me kept me continuously drunk for the next five years, despite the growing signs that what I took for tipsy charisma was in fact repellent, drop-down, pants-pissing craziness, and subsequently what made it so hard to break the habit even when I was in total freefall. It took three rounds of rehab for sobriety to stick. The good news was that I was alive. The bad: my five years of vandalizing my brain chemistry had not, as it turned out, magically cured me of my youthful awkwardness. Instead, I discovered in sobriety that I'd reverted to the self-conscious malcontent I'd been before my forehead met the pavement that first fateful Saturday of college.

The first year of sobriety I remained in a protective crouch, reading, exercising like a madman, working a succession of low-wage "recovery jobs," but really what that amounted to was penance. I was in mourning, marooned in the dead end of South Florida, with nothing but a huge black mark on my record to show for my expensive education (despite nightly blackouts, I'd somehow remained high-functioning enough to earn both a BA and a master's in creative writing). I felt cut off and unspeakably ashamed of the hash I'd made of my life.

And angry. Just as the obscene prevalence of staircases might seem the world's defining characteristic to a recent paraplegic, I couldn't help spotting, everywhere I looked, glamorized imagery of all the high times I was missing out on. Whenever I passed a crowd of my reveling peers, a stinging, rageful loneliness caught me by the throat. Why was I so broken that I needed booze to connect with others? What was my malfunction? Sometimes, I pinned that character defect on my upbringing: a forced march from country to country, condemning me to rootless unbelonging.

It's a wonder that I didn't cave in and relapse, but something unexpected happened first. I began to take a bloody-minded pride in my outsider status. After all my years of yearning to stand apart but lacking the nerve to do so, I *was* special now, if only in the sense that submitting to age-appropriate norms would kill me. With the benefit of a little detachment, I saw how close I'd come to being swallowed by the romanticized cliché of the hard-drinking writer and how close, in early sobriety, I'd come to being suckered by yet another glorified trope: the hard-partying twenty-something, reenacting beer commercials night after unvarying night and mistaking that mass-marketed brand of living dangerously for novelty and adventure.

Just as Carl Jung characterized problem drinking as reflecting "a thirst for spiritual wholeness," my own alcoholism, I grasped, had been a short-cut, however empty and degrading, to transcendence—a means of escaping the dreary confines of myself and the monotony of being, of making contact with something larger and more ecstatic. But there were quieter, more constructive ways of achieving this. Writing, for instance, which about a year into sobriety I returned to. As I sat down at my computer day after day, the act of filling pages felt different than it had in my early twenties: less about the performance of an identity and more about coming to grips with what had happened to me, figuring out what I was put on this earth to say. I kept at it in part because retreating to this solitary, monastic craft for a fix of the transport I'd only ever tasted in my cups felt, in the

FOMO era, like a renunciation of the twenty-first-century imperative to live large and be seen doing it. It felt, in other words, like a radical act of self-cloistering, my own version of churchgoing in the sixties. I sincerely believe it's what kept me alive, if only because in disconnecting from one audience I could connect with another—the imagined reader to whom, in my isolation, I was addressing my work, and whose companionship was all I had in those meager days.

Coming back to writing set me pondering my father's scorn for cliché and received wisdom. What if his contrariness wasn't, as I'd once assumed, just about lording his sophistication over the rubes, but about the insidiousness lurking within even the most benign of platitudes? I began to wonder if a measure of perversity—whose root meaning is "to turn away from the good"—was a survival tactic necessary in a profoundly sick culture where so much of what is extolled as good and desirable happens to impoverish, degrade, and prematurely kill you. Had my father, in his churlish refutation of norms, been practicing his own form of sobriety?

I've heard my dad's stories of his youth so many times that they are often more vivid to me than my own childhood, his hoard of hair-raising anecdotes polished by frequent retelling to a mythic gleam. There were the star-crossed neighborhood kids, forever blowing their fingers off with fireworks, firing guns in the stands at football games, beating each other half to death in the school parking lot with axe handles. There was his abusive, bipolar harridan of a mother, his ne'er-do-well stepfather whom my teenage dad was regularly dispatched to rescue from one dive or another where he'd passed out facedown in a puddle of sour Pabst. There was the next-door neighbor's kid who shot the adoptive parents who had sexually abused him, and the little murderer's brother, whom my grandmother, in a misbegotten gesture of Christian charity, decided to take in. Folly, madness, and nihilism hung thick in the air of Templeton Knowles, Maryland, the grim, godforsaken bedroom community outside Washington DC in which my father grew up.

I'd imagine that, as with so many writers, being starved of affection and affirmation in childhood left my father with a bottomless hunger for love. Ultimately, he channeled that longing into his work. And yet, how would he have turned out had he sought more immediate gratification? He must have intuited that courting approval by adopting the attitudes around him would mean sharing the fate of so many of his family members: poverty, fecklessness, early graves. To save himself, he had to separate himself. And to do so he had to neutralize the power peer and family acceptance held over him by tacking hard in the other direction, throwing himself into a life of the mind that couldn't have been more alien to his peoples' values. That pattern of breaking ranks with those around him—and measuring success in terms of their disapprobation—eventually habituated into second nature, fixing into both an identity and an artistic stance.

In support of my little hypothesis, I can only point to my own misadventures in alcoholism. I, too, suffer from an overwhelming need to be approved of (though mine is rooted in a peripatetic upbringing not an abusive one). But unlike my father, who had the chutzpah to go his own way, I gave into the seductiveness of the herd so cravenly I was nearly trampled.

Surely, drinking myself into near oblivion was also a way of murdering my father's darling—of violently rebelling against my typecasting as the nice, quiet one who doted on his dad, and of poaching market share from the old man's monopoly on the family's attention. Perhaps above all it was a diversionary tactic, a spectacular flameout to create a smokescreen for the more devastating version of failure I feared: discovering I didn't have the goods to make it as a writer, and thus never escaping my father's shadow.

The irony is that in sheering away from my father by means of alcoholic self-destruction, I arrived at a deeper understanding of him. It took my own brush with extinction to see that his childhood had been a near-death experience, and that every day since then he'd been inoculating himself against the contagion of social influence, just as I learned I had to in sobriety. It took forcible removal from the mainstream for me to see that his outrageous flouting of convention didn't stem, as I'd once thought, from an attention-seeking need to be special but a desperate desire to live a life on his own terms. A life in which he was not drawn dangerously off course by looking to others for his cues and validation, one insulated from those pressures that bludgeon us into line at the expense of our well-being (and of good art). Sometimes, I wonder if he has projected and even manufactured an adversarial dynamic with others to perpetuate a narrative in which he is cast as the low-rent, unclubbable outsider, railroaded by the clannish elite. It's mother wit to him, and what drives him, gives him a direction in which to vent his rage. For all the turbulence that default oppositionality has caused him, it's also been an effective life strategy. It enabled him to survive his youth and produce over twenty books, largely out of spite.

I'm now thirteen years sober, and I'm not the mealy mouthed pleaser I once was. In my own work, I'm drawn to problematic subjects—the opioid epidemic, corruption in the financial services complex—that involve rooting around behind the veneer of respectability to unearth unsettling finds. And while my own probing of the dark side has helped me understand that my father's unreasonableness is the kind of resistance that drives the world forward, I've also seen that being an uncompromising renegade has its pitfalls, and I'm not cut out for it. Maybe because I wasn't forged in a crucible of dysfunction but enjoyed plentiful advantages, not least of all loving, supportive parents, I lack the steel to live the permanently embattled existence of the enfant terrible. Then too, I'm a big believer in not burning bridges. Setback and defeat have taught me how hopelessly outmatched I am by life's vagaries and how reliant I am on the wisdom and goodwill of others to get by.

On the evidence, my consensus-seeking MO seems less apt to yield returns; by the time my father was my age, he had six novels to his name. Sometimes that achievement gap haunts me: Isn't it the natural order of things for the son to better the mark set by his father? But there I go with the socially programmed clichés again. In any case, I'd rather not think of my father as a competitor, but as what he has come to be in adulthood: my closest friend and fellow misfit, with whom I've had the most formative conversations of my life, and who, in that maddening provocativeness of his, can always be counted on to show me some aspect of the world I think I know in a new, unexpected, and savagely funny light.

These days, when I hear my dad's dyspeptic tone in my own voice or sense his tendency to rant seeping into my prose, I let it ride where once I might have fretfully self-censored. To the extent that it has filtered down to me, his perversity may just be my richest inheritance. True, his willfulness isn't always easy to stomach. But the fact that he never gave an inch to life's finger-wagging arbiters of rectitude, often at great personal expense, yet bested the demons of his childhood to make an exemplary life for his family, stands to my mind as a triumph of moral courage. If there's a takeaway here, it might be this: Bucking prescription may not make you universally loved, but better to live seeking your own truth than die serving another's. I doubt I'd still be here to muse on that lesson had I not taken a page from the old man's book.

# Off, Off, Off, Off, Off

DANIEL MENDELSOHN

My mother is shutting things off.

It is the day before New Year's Eve in the 1970s, and we are leaving for a weekend at Aunt Alice's house in New Jersey, and as she does whenever she leaves the house, even if it is not for a weekend, even if it's just to drive the mile and a half to the A&P on Round Swamp Road to return a dented can of tuna, my mother has to make sure that the burners on the stove are turned off before we walk out the front door. We five kids are downstairs, slumped on the playroom couch watching *Santa Claus Conquers the Martians*, our eyes glazed with boredom, our skinny legs in their bell-bottoms jackhammering with impatience; upstairs, at the kitchen table, Daddy is anxious to get going. *The traffic, the traffic*, he's saying, closing his eyes and shaking his head with a resigned grimace. *We have to beat the traffic on the Belt Parkway*, but now as always my mother's rituals take precedence over my father's concerns about practicalities. *Off, off, off, off, off*, she says out loud, and with each syllable she briefly places her right hand on a black plastic knob—four for the burners and one for the oven—to make sure it's pointing to "Off."

By this point my father, defeated, has wandered downstairs to join us, and so it's from down there that we all hear her call out, *Jay, children, I'm ready!* And then we file out the front door and pile into the maroon Chevy Biscayne wagon, and Daddy starts the car, and we're on our way to West Orange and Aunt Alice, who has been my mother's closest friend since they were in junior high school in the Bronx together, in the 1940s—my mother's friendships, like her blue-and-white porcelain tchotchkes and her grandmothers' mortar-and-pestle sets, are immaculately curated, pristine, unchanging—and whose rambling house, always filled with noise and the aroma of things baking, we love to be in.

We don't think of Mother's rituals as rituals; they are the medium in which we live, as natural as air. To us and everyone who knows her, my mother is just "very strict" and "very clean." *Wipe your feet or I'll break your legs!* she will shout down to us, cheerily, from the kitchen as we stumble into the front hall after school. We can picture her face as she says this: the brilliant wide smile with its prominent, slightly aggressive canines, the high cheekbones lifted even higher by the grin, the hazel eyes narrowed in apparent amusement, the chestnut flip with its peroxided highlights (*how else will they know I was blond as a child?!*), all springing back from the perfectly triangular widow's peak. It's her movie-star face, the dazzling expression she can instantly assume if someone's about to take a picture. Someone glimpsing her at the moment she says, *Wipe your feet or I'll break your legs!* might think she's joking, but we know how bad things can get if we track dirt onto the carpet.

"Tracking dirt in," "spilling," "making a mess" at the kitchen table: During my childhood these are the worst things that can happen, the things that bring on the shouting and the tears, the incredulous accusations, the *How could you be so careless?* the *Now look and see what you've done!* The things that leave her weeping and half-whispering to herself, as she cleans up the mess on her hands and knees, that this wasn't the life her father had raised her to have. And so she has instituted her rituals and rules— procedures that, when you think of it, are necessary, if you're raising four sons and a small daughter in a modest split-level, two boys to a room, four bedrooms in all, and you want everything, from the bedrooms with their nautically crisp bedspreads to the gleaming white kitchen (where the oven is used to store bread because, after all, baking would get the oven dirty) to the living room with its hieratic displays of porcelain and glass, even to the so-called playroom, where games are rarely played and, if they are, go immediately back into the labeled Tupperware containers the moment they are over. If you live in such a house, there are procedures that must be adhered to if you want everything to stay spotless.

What we had to do was, in fact, called "the procedure." *Do your procedure!* she'd call down to us as we came in the house after school, and we knew what to do: Take off our shoes and bring them downstairs to the basement, where they'd be lined up near the slop sink; go upstairs to our rooms and take off our school clothes, hang them up on the hooks behind our bedroom doors, change into our street clothes, put our homework on our desks, go to the kitchen and fix ourselves milk and cookies at the kitchen table. There was a specific way to do everything: a way to load and then to empty the dishwasher, a way to wash pots and pans, a way to take out the trash, a way to carry the laundry basket down to the basement where the washer and dryer stood, the giant plastic trash cans lined up waiting for their whites, their colors, their delicates, which every day would fill up after we'd carried down the baskets, and every night would empty out again as she did load after load.

We would do this procedure and then we could go out and play while inside, mother would be roaming the house, inspecting the rooms we'd just left. If she was satisfied, she'd go back to the kitchen to sit at the table and enjoy the moment she had each afternoon before she had to start dinner—doing her nails, say, while chatting with Aunt Alice, the phone cradled between her left shoulder and her bent neck so she could keep her hands free, the extra-long cord (*that way I can walk around the kitchen while I talk!*) pooling on the floor at her swollen feet while she filed and poked and polished, holding her hand away from her every now and then and splaying her fingers, like someone trying on a ring.

If she wasn't satisfied, we'd soon know it, even if we were outside playing. I tended not to play with the neighborhood kids as much as some of my siblings did. My older brother, for instance, was part of a group that would regularly organize games of touch football or baseball in the street outside our house, games in which I was not encouraged to take part because I was no good at sports, and in which I was included only when they were desperate to make up a team. On one such occasion,

I was almost enjoying myself—I'd actually caught a pass and run a few yards—when my mother opened her bedroom window, leaned out, and called my name. I went in.

*Do you call this a hospital corner?* she asked. She was standing there, pointing to a spot on my little twin bedstead. *It's supposed to be a right angle.* I shook my head and made it up again.

Not every time she called us in was to rehearse the fine points of making the bed. On some afternoons she'd poke her head out of her bedroom window and say, *Children, children, come inside this instant!* and we'd file in, expecting the worst, but instead she'd be standing next to the kitchen table pointing at an apple or a grapefruit that she'd sliced down the middle. *Look how marvelous nature is* she'd exclaim, pointing to the starlike splaying of the seeds, the elegant outward radiation of the triangular sections. *It's pure geometry!*

On some days when we came in and she'd say, *Do your procedure*, she'd be sitting at the kitchen table sharing her afternoon snack with Mrs. Wilk, our cleaning lady, who'd been coming so long that, as my father liked to observe, not without affection, she did little more after a certain point than share my mother's hard-boiled eggs and tea and gossip about the other ladies on the block. The *pani*, the fancy ladies, Mrs. Wilk would say with a humorous snort as she described the exigencies imposed on her by the neighborhood women—unlike my mother, who, because of her need to have everything perfectly immaculate, would clean the house before Mrs. Wilk came each Tuesday morning, with the result that this stout Polish woman came to see her as a comrade rather than a mistress. They'd sit there, making their tea and eggs last for hours, the housewife and her housekeeper, talking about their husbands and their children and, occasionally, other things. One day in the early 1980s, when I was home on spring break from college, I was wandering from my bedroom toward the kitchen and overheard my mother saying, almost as if to herself, *All I want is for everything to be clean and quiet. But then everyone comes home and it's over.* When I repeated her comment to my father—I'd begun to understand that I could use my mother's mania for cleanliness and order, her rules and rituals, the *procedure*, to ingratiate myself with him—he snorted and shook his head. *But then everyone comes home and it's over*, he repeated; and then, after a pause, *That's what the rest of us call "life."*

Life, we somehow knew, was what filled Aunt Alice's house. There you could take food out of the fridge without needing permission; there Alice would ask if we wanted to help flour the pan or separate the eggs, help assemble the lasagna or roll out the dough for her famous rugelach; there the attic and the basement playroom were spaces into which neither she nor Uncle Sid had any desire to penetrate—a fabulous, unimaginable abdication of parental prerogative, it seemed to me, who had a secret compartment underneath one of my dresser drawers filled with diaries written in code and wrinkled sketches of a certain boy in my homeroom, which my mother would regularly clean and organize, assuring me that she never "looked." At Alice's annual New Year's parties we children ran free, while the adults—the Gang of Five, as we called them, and their husbands; the five girls who'd grown up and then gone to Hunter College together in the early fifties, Marlene and Alice and Marcia and Mimi and Irma, the "girls" still as thick as thieves, the men long grown used to one another, for better or worse—lounged with their glasses of wine or whiskey, my mother telling one of her funny stories, the wide grin gleaming, the slow buildup to the finale, all as carefully crafted and as designed to delight as her displays of delft. When my mother told her stories, or one of the jokes she'd collect and save up for occasions like these, jokes about old Jewish men on their deathbeds, about shtetl rabbis secretly machinating to see what pork tastes like, a light would come into my father's eyes, as if he were recognizing someone he hadn't seen in years. Sometimes my mother would take down her high school yearbook from the carton in which it and some other ancient family documents were carefully stacked and show us the page where her picture appears (*That was my Dietrich phase. I wore men's suits to school. My uncle was a tailor, and he made them for me!*) and where, under "Hobbies," she'd put *spelunking*, and under

"Career Goals" she'd put *taxidermy*. It occurs to me now that when she did this perhaps she, too, was trying to recognize someone.

So my mother would tell her stories, and everyone would laugh, and my father would get that look in his eye. Then, on New Year's Day, we'd drive home, and once we walked in we knew what to do.

Now it is 2018; I am fifty-eight. I'm sitting at her kitchen table, the same white table in the same white kitchen in the same white split-level, imploring my mother once again to come see the house I have bought. I've come home for a brief visit—it's funny, I realize, that I keep referring to the house in the suburbs as "home," forty years after leaving it—and after the usual mournful rehearsal of her friends' and relations' illnesses and operations and Alzheimer's, punctuated every now and then by her wry asides (*Nobody ever just drops dead anymore!*), I try to cheer her up by proposing a week in the country at my place. She sighs.

I didn't buy a home until I was in my fifties, and for a long time I told myself that there were practical reasons for this. I'd been a freelancer for so many years, after all, and was never sure whether I could make that kind of financial commitment, given how erratic my income could be. Manhattan real estate was so crazy, I told myself: renting was so easy. I needed money for the two boys I was helping to raise, I told myself: their tuitions, the vacations, the school clothes. This was the kind of thing I told myself year after year, long after my peers had bought homes, long after my friends had stopped asking why I didn't finally settle down and *own*, long after the stability of my income was no longer a cause for concern. Whether my rationalizations had any validity, I can't say. But I do know that, during all the years I was a renter, I felt free. If I scuffed a floor or put a dent in a wall, it wasn't mine; if something didn't work, a ceiling fixture or air conditioner, I wasn't responsible for fixing it. For most of my adult life, wherever I lived, I felt exhilaratingly unburdened, unconstrained by the implacable demands I had come to associate with houses.

Then, a few years ago, I fell in love with a little nineteenth-century farmhouse at the end of a road near the river and bought it. After a year of renovations—I could have lived in it right away, it's true, but I'd waited so long and I wanted it perfect—I moved in. The boys are grown, I have no pets, I live alone. There is no threat that some small child will crash into my Robsjohn-Gibbings end tables, that some puppy will break the Venini bowl or the Salviati vases. I am happy, I realize. Everything looks *perfect*, people say who come to the house, including my cleaning lady, Chelsea, with whom I spend more and more time talking about our kids, her bright daughter Madison who wants to be a writer, my boys just graduating from high school and college. She likes to joke that I'm so neat she barely has to clean.

It is to this house that, lately, I've tried to get my mother to come for a visit. There are practical barriers, I know. Even when she was young, she never drove very far outside what she called her "driving range": the strangeness of unknown streets and neighborhoods made her panic, and so when we had to go anywhere beyond the little bedroom community where I grew up, it was Daddy who would drive, already muttering his imprecations about the Belt Parkway and the traffic, *the traffic*, while Mother locked up the house. But Daddy isn't there anymore, and so I have offered, again, to drive down from the Hudson Valley to Long Island to pick her up and drive back with her to my place, and then to drive her back down to Long Island again when she's finished visiting. That is how eager I am to show her my perfect house in its perfectly quiet setting. It is a house, I am convinced, that will please her.

But I know she won't be coming. My father died six years ago; we children have long since left Long Island; the Gang of Five has dissolved, dead or dying or cut off by my mother, who, as time passes, has become as intolerant of small differences of opinion as she once was of small dents in cans of tuna. Everything, finally, is clean and neat, and nobody is coming home.

So we have our lunch, gossiping about my siblings, commiserating about her declining friends. Then it's time to leave. Outside, the blue-and-white car from the suburban taxi service is waiting for me; the train station is beyond her driving range. I walk out of the kitchen and down the steps to the front hall, already anticipating the moment when, settled into the back seat of the cab, I will turn to have one last look: the white house, my mother neatly framed by the doorway, making a little wave with the tips of her fingers. I'm putting on my coat when I hear her voice from upstairs. *Off, off, off*, she says softly. Then she bursts out laughing. *Oh Daniel, how funny! I'm doing "off, off, off," but I'm not the one who's leaving!*

# What We Keep

DONNA MASINI

I'm laid up in bed while my friend Medrie, staying with me as I recover from a hip replacement, reluctantly spoons leftovers (who saves oatmeal?) into a Tupperware. I watch her examine the lid, frown, throw it out. I insist she retrieve it. *It's broken*, she explains. I do not correct her. I do not say that "broken" isn't the right word. It's torn. There's an inch-long tear on an otherwise-good five-inch lid. *Just give it to me*, I say.

I could argue it's the painkillers. Or the idea of being helpless while my friend controls "my space." An objective correlative, the psychic reminder of my worn-out hip joint, labral tear. I'm too young for a hip replacement. And what have they done with my old hip, which has always been part of me? But it's the lid. *What*, I demand, *will I use to cover the container?* She pulls it from the trash.

The vehemence with which I attacked my—amused? alarmed?—friend must seem irrational. What could it cost to buy a new lid? But they don't sell lids. And what's a container without a lid? For accuracy's sake, it's not, by definition, a Tupperware. Habit maybe, but I call any food storage receptacle a Tupperware. My mother sold Tupperware.

My mother. On an overnight with my sister, my mother pulls a velvet-wrapped dagger of glass out of her handbag. Her makeup mirror. My sister and I had, on seeing it the year before, bought her a new one. Where was it? What would make someone save such a thing? But I see myself in my mother's alarming mirror: why get rid of something that still works? Hadn't I grown up watching my grandfather repair all manner of things—our rusted window-screens stitched together with spiders of black thread? Didn't everyone glue the handle back onto the paintbrush, wrap it with duct tape? Stick the head back onto the Infant of Prague with a toothpick? Couldn't I glue or tape the lid? Sew it?

Why is it so hard to throw things out?

Last fall, while my mother was in the hospital, I spent ten days in New Jersey with my father. Every time I reached into the closet for a box of pasta, can of tomatoes, some wedding favor or broken figurine would slip from its tangle of yellow ShopRite bags, releasing a cascade of bills, circulars, birthday cards, Bed Bath & Beyond coupons to the floor. *Your mother*, my father would say, as I picked up years-old pharmacy enclosures (my mother *reads* them), clippings—De-germ with Lemon! 25 Uses for Vinegar. How to De-clutter. My father was desperate. He belongs to that tribe—unsentimental, minimalist—who can throw things out. It has been a sixty-two-year struggle. *Do something*, he said.

*It looks like a museum!* visitors exclaim on entering my mother's house. *Your apartment is so neat!* friends tell me. *Such order!* My mother and I do not appear in need of the extreme "tidying up" that a popular Japanese anti-clutter book recommends. We are tidy. And though I have to fight my urge to save, part of me—the internal chaos that makes a person crave order—loves to throw things out (or at least contain them). In this way I am both my mother and my father. It's a dialectic.

*Do something. Get rid of it. Don't tell her.*

I start in the garage, essentially a storage room (the car's kept outside) about the size of my entire apartment, lined with the dressers, chests, credenzas, shelves, cabinets, armoires (did we ever use this word?) from our apartments in Brooklyn, then our house on Staten Island, each crammed with *things*. Behind one door I find the cards: unused birthday cards, anniversary cards, Christmas, Easter, Valentines, Mother's Day (who stores Mother's Day cards *just in case*?): *To a Son, To a Daughter, For a Niece on Her* . . . Here are giveaway blank cards from St. Jude, March of Dimes. Packets and packets of envelopes. My mother could open a gift

shop. She's got boxes of shopping bags, boxes of boxes, embossed nap-
kins, wrapping paper, tissue paper, decorative bows, and rolls and rolls
of ribbon. Candles and soaps in their velvet-lined gift boxes. Here, too,
address labels, notepads—*From the Desk of, To Do! Betty's List!* And more
yellow ShopRite bags. Hundreds.

I've described one compartment. Imagine what lurks in every drawer.
To list it all would upend this essay. Writing is about selecting the significant detail. Tossing the clutter. (Or saving it to another document.)


My mother saved my (our?) umbilical cord. This was the turf of her
first serious argument with my father's mother, who, when she found
it in a jar in the kitchen cabinet, threw it out. She saved our baby teeth.
All four siblings. (*Disaster*, she phoned once to report. *The teeth got all
mixed up.*) I understand this. Since childhood I have found it hard to
throw away a fingernail, my tissue, in a strange place, and used to save
such things until I found a familiar garbage pail. I whispered goodbye
to my hair when my mother cut it. Even now I'm uneasy when I have to
leave it on a salon floor, as I watch the assistant sweep it into a pile of
other hair. Primitive to believe that to leave a piece of yourself in harm's
way is to give someone power over you. To put you, or it, in danger. (But
remember *Rosemary's Baby*?) Magical thinking, the belief that to throw
away a gift is to endanger the giver. As a child I was afraid, not only that I
would die before I woke, but that my things, unwatched, were in danger.
*I pray the Lord my soul to keep. Bless us and keep us.* I didn't want my dolls,
shirts, hairbands, my grandfather's key ring, to be lost or lonely. I said
goodbye to my bed when I went to school. The fear it would disappear?
I would disappear? My parents? *If I should die before I wake.* I prayed
to protect and preserve everyone I loved. I think I believed I could. I
carried that key ring as if it would keep my grandfather safe. When my
sister died, I took her coat and scarves. I will never dry-clean them. I
keep her tissue in the pocket. Now I have her teeth. Our teeth. We've
had them so long. How can I throw them out? I call my sister's daughter
to see if she'll take them.

The garage is overwhelming. I move to my mother's walk-in closet: racks stuffed with suits and skirts she wore to work in the seventies. Maternity clothes she made herself. Dresses she dieted herself into for weddings decades past. Jeans, trousers, blouses, T-shirts, robes, belts, hats, coats, handbags. All but a three-foot section are clothes she'll never wear again. After wedging back several print maxi skirts, I sink to the floor. Here, in a box under other boxes and bags and stacks of storage bins (one containing a dozen Lancôme sample cases with their lipsticks and blushes) is where I find the teeth. I find decades of letters and cards, many from myself, pages and pages written to explain myself to my mother, to separate, distinguish myself from her.

In a corner of the closet, in a drawer of a 1950s end table, I find the clothbound blank book I gave her. *Keep your secrets in here*, I'd written on the flyleaf. *1983*. It's empty. Not a word. But it is as if she has written a giant FUCK YOU! on every page. I'd wanted to give her a place to keep the kinds of reflections that could have helped her. Haven't they helped me, the journals I've kept since I was fourteen? Hundreds, stacked in my closet, the records of dreams, obsessions, confessions, events recorded before they became memories. Part of me feels a thing hasn't happened until I've written it down.

It occurs to me now that perhaps my mother's closet is her journal. A record of who she was, where and when she worked, married, gave birth; of what she wore, when, one by one, her kids moved out. Her closet an elastic sentence, its branching syntax expanding to contain her history of baptisms, communions, dinner dances, graduations. To enter it is as much a violation as if I were to read her diary. It would take empathy to imagine what all these clothes mean to her. Would my mother value my many notebooks, each with its record of study, of poem drafts, its lists of books read, movies seen, museums visited, concerts, plays, etymologies, definitions, recipes, quotations? What would she make of the common-place books, the folders and binders, the organized clippings (25 Uses for Lemons, De-clutter Now!), the meticulous medical notebooks I've kept for friends, for my sister. My sister is dead. My friends have died.

I've saved no one. Why can't I throw the notebooks out? What will happen to them when I die? Perhaps I keep it all as a hedge against ending. How can you end a list? The thing about lists: they continue. How can you die when you still have all these clothes?

When I read that Japanese get-rid-of-stuff book, I thought of my father, who, time and again while I was growing up, moved through our basement on Staten Island in a frustrated fit of throwing out, tossing armfuls of *junk* into trash barrels while I followed behind, pulling them from the garbage: our drawings, finger paintings, "meteorites," to hide them. Decades later, helping my parents move to the house they live in now, I would find them behind my father's workbench. The tyranny of things. Do we possess them? Do they possess us? I begin to see why we say a person is "possessed."

But even my father wouldn't throw out the box of ornaments my siblings and I made in grade school. They're safe in the crawlspace (beautiful word): the Santa my sister fashioned out of a toilet paper roll, cotton, and crayon. We couldn't save my sister, but we can save her Santa. And my brother's wreath—cardboard, cotton balls, tin foil, sparkles—where will it go? I can't explain what I feel about such things, which meant nothing to me then. Does everything, in time, become a madeleine? Does object plus time equal feeling? I'm reminded of the "Time Passes" passage in *To the Lighthouse* when a shawl Mrs. Ramsay casually wrapped about a skull one night is transformed, years later, into *the* shawl—a chilling emblem that haunts the reader.

Why isn't it enough to remember? *The brain is wider than the sky*, Dickinson says, *for one the other will contain.* But it's not enough to hold the past in my head. I want the cotton ball wreath that brings it back. No wonder my favorite part of school trips was the souvenir shop.

Perhaps my mother felt that her broken mirror held, *actually* held, the years and years of her reflections. And when memory goes? Every object has its correlative. Without it, it's just junk.

But how to explain the Tupperware lid?

*I love everything*, my mother said last week. It was Memorial Day. We were discussing the possibility of an independent living apartment, another move, one that would require drastic downsizing. I suggested what it might be like—imagine!—to live in a place in which everywhere you turned you saw something you loved. You saved it because you love it! *I love everything*, she said. I understand. I tell her we'll give it all—the Hummels and silverware, the dishes, couches, chairs, the angel figurines, and the apron I bought her in first grade—to my niece (who still hasn't answered me about the teeth).

The principle of that Japanese book is to get rid of anything that does not bring you joy. But why is *joy* the guiding principle? Why not save the thing that rips your heart open? Why not save what reminds us of our greatest experiences of interiority and solitude, anguish, dread, no matter how painful. Oh God, why not save everything?

Because I live in a studio, one room is every room, and sitting at my kitchen table, I am beside the dresser I've had since I was three. I know which drawers were mine, which belonged to each of my siblings. This chest has moved with me through five apartments over forty years. It has been painted white, turquoise, eggshell. It has been clawed and bitten by three pairs of cats. It's ugly, my friend Daniel says. But he can't see that what he would call its "element of greatness" comes from its history. My history. It is not a great piece. I don't even know that it could be called a "piece." Whether it has a style. Utilitarian? But I remember staring up at the blond wood-grain patterns, which I can still see although my mother "antiqued" it with steel wool, hammer, and paint when I was twelve. Where did they buy it? Some unpainted furniture place? Did they varnish it? If I stripped it now, down through the layers of paint and antiquing, what would I find? The product of some anonymous factory? But I look at it and see how, one Christmas Eve, I tied my sister, brother, and myself, in our rocking chairs, onto its knobs with jump rope to pretend we were reindeer. How rocking and prancing we pulled it down on top of us, then screamed as our ceramic Dalmatian from Coney Island shattered, our fire hydrant bank crashed, pennies rolled across the floor, and our mother raced in from the living room. Why am I writing this? Sentence by sentence I'm back. My sister is alive, my mother young and six months pregnant. I have arrived at what Bachelard calls "the land of Motionless Childhood."

I cannot throw this dresser out. Perhaps, I say to Daniel, I can be buried in it. It's not a preposterous idea. It would be the ultimate repurposing. And that, perhaps, is what writing is. The first time I had a *physical* impulse to write a poem (though I wouldn't have called it a poem) I was nine. We were visiting my grandparents in Brooklyn, the first time back to our old building—the clotheslines and courtyard and vestibule—after having moved to Staten Island. Nostalgia? I don't think so. I ached to *have* it. To keep it. To capture something by trying to put it in words: change, loss, the sense of time passing, how utterly awful and inexpressible it felt. Our familiar home was now *past* and burnished with the glow of this fact. I could try to make something to contain it, the way this jumble of notes, thoughts, memories might become an essay. Is *memoir* etymologically connected to *armoire*? I make a note to look it up.

I've been trying to find a grand unified theory to encompass all the reasons we—my mother and I—hang on to stuff: it still works, I might need it, x gave it to me, it reminds me of, I can use it as a _____, it's part of me, I just can't. Sometimes they bleed into one another. When, years ago, I handed a tangle of gold chains, crucifixes, and religious medals to my dentist so he might melt them into a crown (*I'm a dentist, not a jeweler*), it was partly because I was broke, and because they'd been gifts, and I loved the idea of resurrecting them, carrying the old holiness in my mouth. Primitive, yes, and a practical bit of recycling.

Perhaps it begins with a helpless dread in the face of flux, the inevitable change and loss, that awful impermanence Buddhists urge us to accept. My mother, child of the Depression, whose own mother died when she was thirteen, does save just about everything. What I do is different. I organize. Like a scientist, I categorize and archive and preserve. For this reason I love things that contain other things. Boxes, drawers, notebooks, closets, Tupperware, vials, jars, journals, shelves, bags, folders, binders with "durable" sleeve inserts, handbags with their many zippered pockets. I love the idea of a Container Store. I love words that contain the histories of other words. You'll have noticed that I love parentheses—those little bookends that contain the interruptions, flights of imagination, and association I want to save. I love sentences whose syntax expands to contain more and more of what we accumulate. Perhaps, in my yearning for permanence, I want this essay to contain my childhood. It was not an easy childhood; why so fiercely hang on to it?

That Memorial Day in my parent's kitchen, unable to find a matching top and lid in three drawers of Tupperware, I gathered every container, many of which had been separated from their lids by inches or years, and dumped them on the floor. My mother watched as I tossed whatever was without a lid (or bottom), even if in perfect condition, into the recycling barrel. (I saved a few, just in case.) I even found a lid that was the size of my torn lid. Since I knew my mother would go through the recycling when I left, I took it all home with me on the bus.

The frenzy I felt in the process, the feeling of relief, of calm, I had when all the lids were matched and back with their partners, helped me understand something. The act of organizing calms me. And all the saving—it's anxiety. Every reason I save things goes back to anxiety. This I share with my mother. And its source? We are going to die. We are going to forget. We are going to lose what we most love. And I understand why, as my mother's memory begins to fail, I get irrationally annoyed if she can't remember a high school friend whose mother stole a trench coat from Korvettes. She has been not only the container of my history, but was also, in fact, my original container. And I cannot bear to let it go.

# My Story about My Mother

There is a memory of my mom that I force myself to recall, often. Spe-cifically, when my mom's being a pain in the ass. When she's calling five times a day and her voicemails start with, "When are you going to get over here and get me my [whatever the fuck she wants that day]." Or when she yells at me in front of a cafeteria full of old people for not coming by yesterday even though I was at a gig two time zones away. Or when she answers the door naked, except for a diaper, and says things like, "Get over it. I used to feed you with these."

Here's the memory: It is the summer of 1977 in Philly. Pauline K. Johnson is a skinny high-yellow black woman with a volleyball-sized Afro. She is an undeniably pretty woman, the type of racially ambigu-ous attractiveness that will be all the rage fifty years later. She is young, twenty-seven. I'm younger, around six years old. I look white, and with zero body fat my mom looks like a teen; sometimes, people confuse her for my sitter. When I was a baby, some thought I was literally her doll.

The memory I yank back up, to the present, again and again is of just doing the damn laundry.

Pulling a shopping cart full of clothes to the laundromat, we walk the mile through Germantown past the mix of Victorian mansions now working as apartment buildings, the rowhouses made for a wealthier population that left two generations before. The cart's loose wheels bounce along the uneven slate sidewalk until we get down to the commercial street, which everyone calls The Hollow. It will take me three more decades to realize the name comes from the park across the street, and not the way the area, covered in trash, makes you feel inside. There at the laundromat, through two hours of boredom, lint, and the toxic perfume of fabric softener, my mom reads to me from the picture books she's brought until, after forever, it's done. On the way home, we buy water ice and turkey hoagies. We eat the "wooder ice" first, along the way, before it can melt.

Back home, on the porch, we consume the sandwiches, sip root beer, feel the sun. It's done. We both now have clean clothes and our lives in front of us. I can see, in my mind, her long beige neck, the slight sweat on her skin, the indentation above her sternum. Talking, laughing. Just eating hoagies, sipping root beer. Feeling safe and loved and taken care of. Cars on the busy intersection of Greene and Manheim doing their thing.

At this point, my mom is getting her bachelor's degree, working full-time in the financial aid office at the university. Everything is potential. What I don't know sitting on that porch is I will never be happier. I will, many times, fortunately, be as happy. But I will never be happier, more full than full.

I force myself to think of this memory because I take care of a very different version of Pauline K. Johnson now. This version I take care of is in a wheelchair, an electric one. Multiple sclerosis has diminished her ability to move her muscles, robbed her energy. Dementia has destroyed her brain from the inside out; On scans, it looks like an apple rotting from its core. The version of Pauline K. Johnson I know now will sometimes call me hourly, forgetting she called earlier, seeing my one returned call then calling five more times to see what I was calling about. This version is incontinent, can be petulant, teeters between helplessness and willful dependence in a way I have to constantly negotiate, the line between assisting and enabling always uncertain. Pauline K. Johnson is still Pauline K. Johnson: funny, profane, kind, selfish, utterly devoted to me, my mom. We still go for walks, but it's me walking her, and if I'm not careful, she will roll over my damn toes, which she finds hilarious. So she is like herself, but also like she's just slammed back a whole bottle of wine, or time-warped into the mind of herself as a toddler.

The version I know now kicks my ass. I am her sole caregiver, her only child. This version sometimes makes me cry in my car after I've left her, or scream as I drive away. This version breaks my heart because I remember the other versions of Pauline K. Johnson, the healthy ones, better than she does now.

When my mom left my father, I was four. I didn't see her for two weeks. When she finally showed up again, she picked me up from daycare and let me buy a new toy from the corner store—an unprecedented event. Before then, most of my toys came either on holidays or from the clear plastic grab bags at the Value Village Thrift Store. But on this day, while picking up toiletries downtown for my stay at her new apartment, she let me get a green plastic frog, a windup to place in the tub. Afterward, we took the Number 34 trolley to her new place in West Philly, a bedroom she was renting in her girlfriend's apartment.

We were passing by Clark Park in University City, still a mile from our destination, when the trolley stopped, stuck behind traffic. We got out, walked, found the reason for the hold up. Two blocks up, cop cars everywhere, police lights flashing. Someone had robbed the corner pharmacy. As we crossed the intersection, a cop came out of the corner store guiding a man by his arm.

The man held his palm to his face, his fingers wide like he was holding a basketball. Beneath those digits, blood pouring. A face with no features, just a mass of pulp held together by his grip, blood dripping down the brown of his arm to the asphalt.

"What happened?" I asked.

"He got his face blown off," my mom told me. "They're taking him to the hospital. He'll be okay." She covered my eyes with her hand.

I thought that the man had no face. That it was simply *blown off*. That he had a stump instead of a nose or lips or a brow, and his hand was the only thing keeping his brain from falling out.

And even with that interpretation, I saw him get into the ambulance, and thought, *He'll be okay.* That he was going to the hospital, so therefore it would all work out.

One morning in the fall of 1977, my mother woke up, but half her body didn't. Left side. Just didn't work. Right down the middle, between the eyes. Limp, paralyzed. It was two years since her divorce, I know I was seven years old, but I don't know where I was in that moment, and this is one of the many things that my mom doesn't remember anymore. What she does recall is dragging the limp half of her body from the bed to the floor, to call for help. Ernie, this goofy red-haired white guy she briefly dated, had a blue Ford F150. She called him. After she had hung up, she realized that the front door was locked. She was in the back of the house, on the second floor.

My mom dragged herself down the hall, pulling herself with her one hand. At the top of the flight, she got her legs in front of her, and bounced down on her butt one step at a time. She was some kind of tired. She would remain feeling some kind of tired for the rest of her life, really.

Ernie was a twenty-five-minute drive away, and he made it to her front door before she could. She heard the sound of him knocking as she lay on the living room floor, trying to will herself the rest of the way.

They didn't let me see her for nearly a month. The adults. But they whispered about her around me, my dad glancing in my direction, concerned that I might hear grown-up truth. I didn't know what the hell was going on. I was smart enough to know that they were hiding information, but too ignorant to be scared.

At seven, I thought when you went to the hospital, you always got better. That was my complete understanding of the world. I figured if they could fix that dude with his face blown off, my mom had nothing to worry about it. Now, at forty-seven, every time I hear an ambulance siren, I think, *Someone's life just changed forever.*

When my father finally brought me to see her, we met her in the lobby of Lankenau Medical Center in the wealthy Main Line, across the Schuylkill River and a world away from Germantown. The nurse rolled her into the lobby; I'd never seen my mom like that.

In a wheelchair, her right side still weak. Her mouth still drooped a little on that corner, and it would do that for the rest of her life when she was tired. She would come home from work and smile joylessly in the mirror. Touching the sides of her lips to see if it was drooping again.

Meeting me in the lobby of the hospital, she brought a box of chocolates the size of a hatbox resting on her lap. I ran to her, hugged her like I could pick her up and carry her out with me, and knocked all those chocolates to the floor. We both watched that box wobble; she couldn't do anything to stop it.

When the chocolates hit the linoleum, the cone-shaped ones rolled in concentric circles. The loops getting wider and wider as we stared. I watched them roll, and I watched her, stuck in her wheelchair. And that's when I figured it out. The gravity of what was going on. That's what it took for me to understand that she couldn't take care of herself.

Eighteen years later, I wrote my first novel. Like most first novels, it was awful. My girlfriend at the time read it and diplomatically said, "Well, I really loved this one scene." The chocolates story, which I'd recalled verbatim.

This is how I learned to be a writer, that the only way I could create anything worth reading was to chop myself into bite-sized pieces and serve them raw like sashimi.

I learned how to write better books, to make a living off of this, and off of teaching others to do the same. And I tell the chocolates story to my fiction students, sometimes. To show them that to truly know something, you have to experience it. To explain to them that story is how we learn and store information. That storytelling is an attempt to replicate the operating system of the human brain. That what we are doing as fiction writers is creating experiences outside the reader's own life for them to explore. I usually do this lesson at the beginning of term. When I do it, I often find myself on the verge of tears by the end of the tale. This is great because it teaches them you have to truly care about what you're writing. It also teaches them that I'm a little loco, so don't fuck with me.

Pauline K. Johnson rose from that wheelchair after a few months in the hospital and got on with her life. Eventually, she walked out the hospital doors. There are two primary kinds of MS: the kind that hits you hard and keeps getting worse and the kind that comes and then backs off for a while—the relapsing/remitting. And my mom got lucky. A few weeks after that lobby visit, she was back in her house, in remission.

We didn't even talk about it until much later, what had happened. Like it was bad luck, like the MS might hear us and come back again. Sometimes she would tell me that her friends, her lovers, were scared of her now. That lurking behind their friendship was the fear that someday, they would be forced to take care of her. I always thought that was odd, paranoia. I didn't realize that burden was destined to fall on me instead.

My mother's name is Pauline K. Johnson; she was married to my father for only seven years but has kept his name for five decades. This is partly because her father was an abusive asshole, and partly because what's in a name anyway? She is of course an individual and should be named as such, but she is "mother" or "mom" to me. Her role in my life remains so overwhelming that I have to force myself to write her actual name, Pauline K. Johnson, to remind myself that she exists outside of me, although it didn't feel like that when I was a child, utterly dependent on her, and it doesn't feel that way now that she is utterly dependent on me.

The word *Mom* is both intimate and generic. It speaks of the history and intensity of our relationship, but also that there are major parts of her to which I will never have access, by situation, by her choice, by mine. Pauline K. Johnson is not married, has no other children, no one else in the world day to day but me. *Mom* is a title and once it was her job, but now it declares my responsibility.

My mom was healthy for so long, we started to second-guess the original diagnosis. For twenty-two years, the symptoms were quiet enough to confuse silence for absence. For another decade she raised me, went to work, came home, collapsed facedown on the bed diagonally because that's the angle the door was to the mattress. Planking, she'd call for me and I'd come pull her boots off. Two hours later, she'd get up, cook me a burger and mixed vegetables because that was the only thing I would eat. I swear, two decades of a diet of growth-hormone-enriched beef is why I grew six inches taller than anyone in my family tree.

My father was always in the picture, emotionally, financially, every other weekend and two weeks in the summer. But mostly, it was me and her. Every day, in the apartment, her smoking True Greens, utterly unaware of secondhand smoke. Talking to friends on a phone whose cord was like a dragon's broken spine, talking to one after another for three hours because that was her primary social outlet. Both of us watching TV, every night from 6 to 11 p.m., until I hit eighteen.

Single mom and son. As a hetero male, I've had female lovers in my life reflect on this dynamic, usually in the form of complaint, or critique of how the intensity of the single mother-son bond can become toxic after the transition to adulthood. Of the suffocating codependence it can form. The stories of adult sons and the mothers who refuse to emotionally cut the cord. I know there is sometimes truth to this; I get it, I do. I also know, unless your experience is the one parent—one child family unit, it's impossible to describe the bond that is created, the level of intimacy produced by having your life utterly indebted to one person. One person who fed you, nursed you when you were sick, protected you when you were weak, gave you your first glance of the world through their eyes. Sacrificed the other lives they could have had without you in the hope that you might have an even better one.

When I went to college, Pauline K. Johnson went to Alaska. I was experiencing freedom, and she, no longer stuck in the role of full-time mom, wanted the same. This was the first time we were truly apart. Me at school and later living off and on in the United Kingdom. Her in Kotzebue, a small town in northern Alaska accessible only by plane. It was an abrupt break from our little apartment for two, but I still depended on her emotionally.

Terrified of being alone in the world, I got engaged to a woman I barely knew, then got dumped not long after. Heartbroken and feeling broken in general, stuck in South London cut off from anyone whom I hadn't just met. I cried to my mom on the phone like the child I still was in many ways, the long-distance call complete with pre-digital two-second delay. Two weeks later, I received an express envelope sent all the way from her Arctic village. It was filled with pictures of family members, neighborhood friends. Her letter said, "These are photos of people who love you."

In the last decade, I have watched my mother's body succumb to the destiny foretold. I've seen the scans of her brain, the growing number of scars from MS's cerebral blisters, perfect white circles on the imaging that remind me of mint Life Savers. I've seen her go from a cane to a mobility stroller to a wheelchair. Her control of her body loosens; the MS has affected muscles I took for granted. Her weakened throat slurs her speech and makes her cough desperately when she eats. Lack of muscular control in her groin means a lack of bladder control, and constant incontinence makes going anywhere a risk for social catastrophe. Her brain has good days, but mostly bad ones. She can remember something she wants from me forever (to go to Red Lobster, to get a new sundress, to buy whatever miracle pill she saw advertised on TV), but other basic details elude her. On occasion, she has delusions, like that she's going to ride a bike again. Her vocabulary has been reduced; she can talk and certainly has tons of creative requests for me, but often "that's nice" becomes her constant conversational response. "Oh wow" she reserves as a response for the best information.

Twenty minutes from my house, my mom lives in a senior apartment building where the staff cooks and cleans for her. She has a helper three days a week. I see her at least one day a week and stress about her situation and what might be ahead the other six days.

Pauline K. Johnson now lives through me. I control her money, her medical treatment, her future. I buy her everything she needs. I am her primary source of transportation, entertainment, support, companionship, love. If I let her, she will take these things from me endlessly, until I am an emotional husk. So I have to set limits. I will go over to her place and bring her things, from medical supplies to a bucket of KFC. There are times that isn't enough for her, and she will verbally attack me. I know, even if she doesn't, that she's largely attacking her situation. The tragedy of her body. That everyone in her building is both significantly older and cognitively more coherent than she is. That people her age, seventy, are out there still working and traveling the world and have bodies that still basically do the same things they did when they were young.

I know I would not be dealing with all of this as well as she is, if I were her. I know I don't deal with it particularly well just being me. I know what she gave me: life. I know there is nothing I can do to repay her, because no matter what I do I can never give her life back to her. I simultaneously know that my guilt about not being able to change this is absurd while also living with the guilt that I'm not doing more. With a constant state of fear about the fact that she's going to get worse, and what if I can't carry the weight?

When I write a fictional story, there is a beginning leading to an end. The beginning presents an emotional conflict, and over the course of the narrative, the characters negotiate said conflict, experiencing and learning as they head toward a conclusion. This conclusion is often defined by their success or failure to negotiate that central conflict. The story attempts to mimic how real life is processed by the human brain.

But real life is not contained by the human brain. Because real life doesn't give a fuck about the human brain. And sometimes, real life will even fuck with the human brain, destroying it with blisters that on CAT scans look like mint Life Savers.

True Story: My mother's body is slowly slipping into paralysis. Her mind is slowly eroding. Things will never get better. The only good part is that as she slips away she becomes less cognizant of this reality. I will always be responsible for her, and always petrified that the next level of her dependence is the one that breaks me. When she eventually goes into full-time care, I will have less physical responsibility, but far more financial. The only conclusion will be in her death, or mine, and there is nothing to negotiate about this but the acceptance of this reality.

And this is also true: as long as Pauline K. Johnson is alive, I have some piece of that first version of my mother, the woman with the root beer and hoagies. The current version of my mother, the one whose diaper I have to change and who called me eight times just yesterday, is also the woman I've always loved, a woman who is still here, yet I miss desperately.

# Never Have Just One Boss

SUSAN ITO

When I was a child, my heart swung on my father's comings and goings from our house. He was a traveling salesman, or as he preferred, a manufacturer's rep. I sat on my parents' bed and watched him pack his suitcase for another thousand-mile, three-week trip from our home in Northern New Jersey through Virginia, the Carolinas, Georgia, Tennessee. He would hit up every gift shop on I-95, hawking cheap souvenirs like collector spoons with state crests on the handles, miniature lava lamps, and pennants with neon images of Stone Mountain and the Great Smoky Mountains. In preparation, he folded his V-necked undershirts, his wide ties, and his plain black belts and socks. I sat cross-legged and handed him items off his nightstand: his tin of Cuticura ointment, a bottle of Old Spice, and an oval brush, like the kind used on horses.

"I'm taking off like a big old bird, Sus," he'd say. He tucked in a few rectangles of cardboard, the kind that came inside his shirts, on which he kept a meticulous spreadsheet, in infinitesimal ballpoint script, of his expenses for gas, hotels, and meals. He used a Parker pen and pocket-sized spiral notebook for notes on customer visits. He fastened two little pins to his label: one from the Freemasons and another, a hand holding up a torch from the 442nd, the U.S. Army's Japanese American regiment during World War II.

"Go for broke!" I knew the motto of the 442nd. I'd seen the black-and-white movie starring Van Johnson amid a platoon of Nisei soldiers. Decades before *The Joy Luck Club* or *Crazy Rich Asians*, I knew what a rare miracle it was to see actors who resembled my father and uncles as the majority of the cast. I was convinced that my father was one of the extras in the film, sure that I saw him crouched in a foxhole, his hundred-pound radio on his back.

After the war, he worked as Bell Laboratory's first Asian American lineman. Later, he got a job with a Japanese import company, but soon found that buyers for fine Imari porcelain were few and far between. It was more lucrative to sell cheap trinkets to souvenir shops up and down I-95.

"Don't forget this!" I'd hand him a miniature photo album, stuffed with wallet-sized photos of me and my mother. He'd show it to customers who were hundreds of miles away, people we'd probably never meet. Instead of a framed photo on an office desk, he kept this album in his briefcase. People all over his territory knew from these photos that he and my mother were Japanese Americans and that they had an adopted, racially ambiguous daughter named Susan. He'd slide it in and lean on his leather suitcase to fasten the brass closure.

He was going on the road, and he'd be gone for weeks, while my mother and I subsisted on frozen TV dinners and Burger King. He drove up and down the interstate in a Mercedes, which I didn't realize was a fancy car until years later. His car looked more like a traveling junk heap to me—packed like a puzzle with cardboard cartons and sample cases of cheap cloisonné jewelry, wrinkled bed sheets concealing it all. He'd printed "NO RADIO" on a ragged piece of cardboard that he carefully fitted over the dials of the high-end sound system. In arm's reach, a plastic baggie filled with hard candies to keep him awake during long stretches of highway. He was a loyal customer of Hickory Motors in North Carolina. Every year, he traded in his car with over 100,000 miles on it, and they gave him a new Mercedes for just a slight increase in price. "They take care of me," he said.

I often wondered why my father went so far, why he stayed away so long. His territory stretched from Richmond, Virginia, through Georgia and Tennessee, with gift-shop customers in cities such as Charlotte, Atlanta,

Gatlinburg, Charleston. I didn't understand why he was different from other fathers, who took the train to Manhattan every morning and came home to our little town every night.

I pleaded with him to move us to Charlotte, North Carolina. Charlotte had Krispy Kreme donuts and my pen-pal friend, Donna, whom I'd met at the annual Gift Show. People in Charlotte spoke in honeyed accents and called me "Darlin'." But it wasn't until much later that I understood that the South was the least favored territory—it involved more driving and less revenue. My father had requested work in New York or New Jersey, but he never got it. Why couldn't we move down South? "Our people are here," was his answer. Our extended family, our Japanese American church in Manhattan, our community. There was no such community in Atlanta or Charlotte.

When I was in elementary school, Dad worked a few wondrous years for Determined Corp. This company held the licensing for Peanuts products: my stuffed Snoopy dog, flannel pennants that said, "Happiness Is a Warm Puppy," small square books with Snoopy and Charlie Brown on the covers, and Joan Walsh Anglund products—dolls, calendars, and little books, like *A Friend Is Someone Who Likes You*, featuring children with just dots for eyes, no noses or mouths. I adored it all. My father had even met Charles Schultz, and every time I saw the comic strip in the Sunday paper I felt a proud sense of ownership, a connection to the source. A banner saying, "I Think I'm Allergic to Morning," hung over my bed, with a bedraggled Snoopy drooping on his doghouse roof. The day my father told me he was parting ways with Determined, it broke my heart.

"WHYYYYY?" I wailed.

"They offered me a full-time job," he shrugged.

I was stunned. Wasn't that a good thing? Why would he *not* want to work for them full-time?

"Because then they own you, Sus," he said. "If they decide to fire you, you're out of a job for good. You're left with nothing."

I was perplexed. "They're not going to fire you! You're the best salesman!"

He spoke slowly, stirring his coffee with a spoon that bore the seal of the state of Georgia. "Listen. Right now I work for twelve companies. I'm a free man; I work on commission. I make *good* commission. That's why they want to put me on salary—they're paying me way too much. There's no way their salary could touch what I make." He stopped to pat my shoulder. "I'm sorry, Rascal."

I pouted. "Do we get to keep the samples?"

Of course. We always got to keep the samples. Which was why he first walled in the sun porch off the dining room, and then he walled off the patio underneath it, and why we could never fit a car into our garage or furniture in the basement. They were all filled, floor to ceiling, with towers of sample cartons, holding merchandise from every company he ever sold for.

The companies shifted through the years. He repped for a porcelain manufacturer in Sebring, Ohio. Glassware, mugs, ashtrays bearing decals with the insignia of a state or tourist attraction. The hippie-esque Paul Marshall Products, with its flower-power decals, incense, wicker furniture and trunks, baskets. Shackman doll furniture and china-headed dolls in christening gowns. Knockoff cloisonné and turquoise jewelry. Samples were jammed into every nook and cranny of our house. My girlfriends loved to come over and burrow through the towers of cartons like treasure hunters—my father was generous with his discontinued samples and let them take away whatever they liked.

While I was in college, I searched for and found my birth mother, and I discovered that she, like my parents, was second-generation Japanese American. By surprising coincidence, she was also a manufacturer's representative like my father, and they had unwittingly crossed paths at gift shows. The next year, he showed up at her Frisbee booth with a box of takeout sushi. I was astounded when he called to tell me they had shared lunch and chatted about their mutual daughter.

When I graduated from college with a degree in physical therapy, I took a cross-country road trip, directionless, until I landed in California and decided to try out the West Coast. The first job I found was per diem, or by the day. I worked in two hospitals, one in Berkeley and one in San Francisco, shuttling back and forth across the Bay Bridge. I worked weekends. I worked holidays and whenever they needed me. I was full of energy, and I loved coaxing my patients out of bed for their first postoperative footsteps. After a while, one of the rehab directors offered me a full-time position. I hesitated. I thought about my dad. *Never have just one boss.* I declined the job and kept patching together weeks of work at a time. Back then, in the eighties, it was easy to buy health insurance for seventy-five dollars a month. Like my father, I let some jobs go and took others on.

I worked as a school-based pediatric therapist and coordinated a nonprofit program called the Committee for Health Rights in Central America. On weekends, I marched in rallies against the U.S.-sponsored war in Nicaragua, collected donated crutches to send to Central America, and went to continuing education programs about how to make lightweight cast boots for children with cerebral palsy.

I moved on to home-based physical therapy, visiting patients where they lived. During those years, I felt even more like my dad, working from the road, my trunk crammed with walkers and stretchy TheraBands for home exercise programs. Instead of driving through a network of Motel 6s, I followed an app on my phone that located all the Starbucks in my territory, where I'd fuel up on caffeine between patients and type Medicare reports on my laptop. Instead of his shoebox full of tattered road maps, I had my trusty GPS with its lilting British accent.

Later, I earned an MFA in creative writing and added writing and teaching to the mix. I taught as an adjunct at community college while directing a camp for adoptive families. Health benefits were not part of my employment packages, but by then I was covered by my husband's insurance; it was a gift to not have to worry about it.

When he was seventy-five, my father suffered a catastrophic aortic aneurism. Emergency surgery saved him, but he was rendered paraplegic and unable to drive; his traveling salesman days were over. My mother drove the Mercedes back to Hickory Motors. When they inspected the car, the driver's window was jammed; they found it stuffed with envelopes full of small bills, totaling five grand. This was cash he made from selling extra samples at the end of gift shows.

My mother and I hadn't known about his hiding place inside the panel of the car door. I realized that my father was a money squirreler. He didn't trust the banks and wouldn't keep his funds in one place. Around the house, plastic bags and dirty cartons marked FISHING GEAR often contained bags filled with random piles of cash. Whether this behavior was leftover from growing up during the Depression or otherwise not fully trusting The Man, he kept his money in a variety of places.

"How's your work, Sus?" my dad would ask during our weekly phone calls. "Doing any physical therapy?" Now that he was a seasoned rehab patient, he was a little wistful about the health profession I seemed to have abandoned. He'd spent years on the road to proudly pay for my education. It had been a long time since I'd seen the inside of a hospital, but I had strong opinions about the physical therapists who progressed him from bed-bound to wheelchair and left it at that. I urged him to apply for benefits at the Veterans Administration; there, they treated him like the soldier he'd once been and pushed him to his goal of getting back on his feet with braces and crutches. He was glad to be back in boot camp.

Even when he couldn't drive, he kept working. He used the phone and conducted business from the kitchen table. After four decades, his customers had come to trust him and only him. Whatever he wanted to sell them, they'd take it. He wasn't your typical salesman. He didn't drink; he didn't fool around. One of his favorite sayings (albeit untrue) was, "We don't make any money, but look at the fun we have." He did have fun, and he was a living manifestation of the promise that if you did what you loved, the money would follow.

Dad was eighty-one when a checkup revealed that the aneurism, a fragile balloon below his heart, had returned. He'd need more surgery. He carried a briefcase to the hospital and made phone calls to the Busch Gardens gift shop from his hospital bed. We were devastated when he died during the operation.

The funeral director gasped when he heard that my father was a veteran of the 442nd. "I'm honored to have one of those heroes," he said, and he ordered a veteran's flag to be presented to my mother.

My mother continued to receive checks, for years after Dad's death, from dozens of posthumous sales. His customers, from gift shops through the South, were filling out their own order forms, sending them in, and insisting that the commissions go to my mother.

*Never have just one boss. Look at the fun we have.* How deeply I took those words to heart. I worked for over thirty-five years as a part-time employee, juggling the teaching, physical therapy, and nonprofits along with parenting two daughters and caring for my aging parents.

My dad was able to stay ahead of the game, back in his day. This gregarious salesman managed to buy a home, buy a new car every year, and pay for my private college tuition, all on commission from selling trinkets. Health insurance was affordable and plentiful, so different from the inadequate, crippling system of today.

"We don't make any money, but look at the fun we have" is now a sad punch line. I wonder what he would have made of so many folks in the gig economy now, with millions of Americans being on the outside of job security and a salaried existence. I think about how lucky he was to actually thrive in his independent, cobbled-together life.

Years after my adoptive father's death, I met the family of my genetic father. He had been a biology professor and his sister an English teacher. She welcomed me warmly into the family and gifted me with one of the only keepsakes her brother had left behind: an antiquated microscope from his graduate studies. I consider the mysterious strands of DNA that may have nudged me toward the sciences in my physical therapy career, the love of literature and writing that I may have inherited from my aunt. Maybe these have also been factors in my ever-changing rotation of jobs and passions—nature and nurture the many bosses of this kaleidoscopic life.

# Spending the Sparkle

JANE HAMILTON

My mother, who has never exercised on purpose in her life, except under duress in gym class and at Girl Scout camp, is an Olympian when it comes to charm. She is a sparkler, "a cocktail," my husband's teetotaler aunt once dubbed her. Which offended me, a term that seemed to trivialize my mother's talents. But I can understand why an acquaintance might think she was all fizz and fun, a pink beverage in a clear cold glass: take a sip and you yourself might become silly.

It's scientifically verifiable that genetics is 100 percent responsible for the sprinkling of charm dust at birth. Following that dusting, charm often creates the space for luck, luck a lurking thing that loves a vacuum. Here's the kind of luck that used to happen to my mother with some frequency: It's 1973, *Uncle Vanya* is on Broadway. The revival is directed by Mike Nichols, the production stars George C. Scott, Julie Christie, Lillian Gish—for God's sake—the First Lady of American Cinema, the silver screen legend. The run has been sold out forever; there is no chance of getting a ticket, forget it. My mother goes to New York anyway. It's not as if she has her own income or spare cash; my parents are comfortable but careful, every expense recorded in a ledger book. She's been at home raising five children. Midwestern housewives of this era do not typically visit the travel agent to book a flight out of Dodge. But to sit tight in Chicago while the theatrical equivalent of the Second Coming is taking place would be to ignore the Star of Bethlehem, to close the shades and go to bed.

She lands in the great city, she goes immediately to the theater, to the box office, she sits in the long window looking out to the street. There must be a ledge, something of a lip. All day she sits there. Right before the curtain goes up a man appears. She later describes him in the hyperbolic way that feels true: the white knight cantering up on a steed. He wonders, Does she need a ticket? She does? Wonderful! No, he won't accept payment; he'd like her to have the seat with his gratitude.

I don't know that she did anything at all to inspire his interest, his generosity, except to be present and be herself. Real charm does not have to insist or ooze; charm, like love, can be patient, can on occasion be still and small. So, she sees the play, she goes home, she writes about the experience on the off chance that a newspaper or magazine might publish it. The essay is a piece of joy that launches a career, a cottage industry. For the next decade she writes about theater people for the *Chicago Daily News*, and other papers regularly run her column too. She flies to New York and London so often it seems impossible to keep track of her. It would be easier to list what actors she did not interview in that period. Anyone who was anyone gladly submitted to her beam. Through the years she received many thank you–love notes; she charmed her subjects in person and then in print.

My mother's thermostat for happiness is set very, very low. She is simply a happy person. Currently she is ninety-seven and in the dementia unit, locked up. Even if she wanted to, she couldn't get on the elevator, papered over to seem like a wall, since she cannot stand or walk. When the exercise matron sends a balloon her way during Sit and Be Fit, her skill at batting the balloon with a florescent solid-core pool noodle deserves an A. She does have that bit of athleticism.

Last summer she contracted pneumonia, and that was it, we figured. We gathered around the bed, we cried, we told her how wonderful she'd been as a person and mother, we read the interviews she'd written out loud. *Look who you met! Al Hirschfeld. Robert Redford. Most of the Redgraves. Anthony Hopkins. THE LUNTS!* It was her goal in those pieces to make every artist, every star she interviewed, look good even if they were jerks. Her essays, models of clarity, brimmed with exuberance.

There we are, marveling at the essays, telling her how goddamn charming she is, and how everyone loves her, a true fact: she inspires love in others without even meaning to, without knowing she is doing it or has accomplished that feat. (Only very occasionally does someone seem exasperated by herself, the cocktail.) There are reasons for her popularity beyond her innate charm. She's an excellent conversationalist, asking questions, listening, taking a sincere interest. Plus, she's good at word play, she can riff, and she's beautiful. She's tall, her limbs and hands are long and graceful, her hair is a shiny silver, and her skin is still pink, not degraded by moles or warts or deep wrinkles.

Weeks are passing when my mother is dying. Then, without medical intervention, she starts to get better. What the hell? We've said goodbye, we've been tender, grief-stricken, I've written the obituary and the eulogy. She continues to improve. My siblings and I, we are actually privately thinking, *What in FUCKING hell?* How can a person be so hale and so hearty when she has never, not ever followed the Thou Shalt Exercise commandment? This is not natural—this is freakish. My mother, the freak of nature. Sure, she ran around when she was caring for five children, up and down the stairs, carrying great heaps of laundry, bending, squatting, pushing a buggy, pushing a heavy roaring Hoover. It's clear there is a lot to be said for the physical benefits of a housewife's routine. (As far as mental health, housewifery has been proven now and again to lead to insanity.) There was a period when she rode a bicycle a few blocks every day, wearing a skirt, a girdle, and green Keds. I am the baby of the family, and when I was a middle-aged child and she was at last freed up, she'd walk a mile or two; there was that. She periodically went to fat camp in Wisconsin for a few days. Because, in addition to not exercising, she loved to eat. Fanny Mae buttercreams—couldn't get enough of them. She still can chow down a hunk of tenderloin and a heap of buttered mashed potatoes, not to mention a slab of chocolate cake. On occasion, she'd go on a diet, or she'd get herself to the Wooden Door, nutrition the focus at fat camp rather than exercise.

How is any of this fair? When I was raising children, only two of them, but also exercising those same mother-muscle groups as my mother had done, I'd additionally go down to the basement and ski my brains out on the NordicTrack. Or I'd go for a five-mile run, much of it on hilly terrain. Or I'd ride my bike for three hours. Is my mother battery operated? Is my freak-of-nature mommy immortal?

Back to my thesis that exercise impacts a person's charm quotient, and let me say here, impacts it not in a good way. If I were to write an essay about someone who is clearly a jerk, I wouldn't protect him or her from her own character. The fact that I don't want people to look better in print than they are—is it the exercise? Has exercise taken the fizz out of the cocktail that is me? Did I receive the full complement of my mother's gift, the same amount originally in the holding tank, and have I in effect squandered it?

My jock genes are from my father, no mystery there. Also body type. I'm a compact little workhorse of a girl animal. I climbed Mt. Rainer with him when I was fourteen. At sixty I did a bike trip in the Pyrenees, on terrain where the Tour De France fellows practice for the big ride. I've done sprint triathlons. You get the picture. It is in my nature, like a workhorse or a collie, to move, to run, to soldier on. Not only because it's a kind of work, but because often exercise is joyful. I would become a lunatic if all I could do was bat at a balloon with a solid-core pool noodle. Yes, it's a different era, we baby boomer women an alternate breed from our 1950 housewife mothers simply by virtue of the girl-power time we live in. It's not a small thing that remarkable female specimens now dazzle the reader in magazine ads, women who are supposedly like the rest of us, their sleek tummies exposed and their little shorts, one drinking her energy beverage on a bike, or radiating comfort in her exercise bra during the marathon, or careening over a hurdle in miracle shoes. However: those ads would not have moved my mother. If she could have chosen otherwise, she would have said, No, thank you. She is not at all sorry to have missed climbing peaks and riding a bicycle up a mountain.

My primary question remains: Does the hard grim brutal work of physical engagement leach from a person a lightness of being? Or is that merely my excuse for not exercising the charm portion of my inheritance? I know I've got the stuff in some measure: I've watched myself flirt shamelessly, as my mother does with just about anyone she encounters. I, too, have a similar capacity for happiness, I am also a writer, I am shallow and have depth in about her same measure, we both avoid cleaning the house, and like her, I can be the personality in the room, the theatrical loudmouth. I am about as close to her, outside the body type, as much a clone as a daughter can be. And yet, I don't inspire instant love; I've never been cast in any play I tried out for, unlike my mother who was in community theater productions into her eighth decade. This has to do with talent, of which I have none, but additionally the hard-bitten quality that I've acquired and Miss Lazybones never did. I've never talked the IRS guy out of a fine, a policeman out of a ticket, nor have I out of the blue been put into first class.

I think about the hard-core ballet training I had as a girl, how grueling it was, lying on the floor of the studio, a fellow student pushing one leg up past my shoulder, the pain of it, the damage that was happening, fiber by fiber, to my hamstrings. We were little marines in service to beauty, and we were tough. I think that kind of discipline and the stoicism required, and the humiliation that a ballet master inflicts upon the student, drives you into yourself. It prepares you, too, for further feats that require fortitude. It may cultivate in you a no-nonsense approach to life, and possibly make you mean.

My mother can be cheerfully stoic, but she is not particularly disciplined. When she had a hip replacement, the physical therapy for her was almost unendurable. Taking a step, using a walker. Taking another step. Her life with the helter-skelter exercise of raising children had not prepared her for rehab, including the extremely mild task of walking in a deliciously warm water pool between parallel bars. You'd think she was being asked to do an Ironman.

"Your mother," one of the trainers said, "is longing to be dependent."

Happiness in its full flower reigns now that she is permanently seated in her throne.

So, maybe I have hoarded my charm, or I've spent it pedaling up steep hills. If a person had a choice, though, say you could choose, I'd rather be charmless and mobile. I'd rather not have winsomeness to spare for the dementia lockup—although my mother's temperament gets her a long way with her caretakers in the joint. Still, if it comes to the lockup for me, I'll hope to see the elevators for what they are; I'll hope, when no one is looking, to board that train, and press Down. *I'm just going outside and may be some time.*

In the meantime, before that luck or horror, whichever way you see it, there was the Mark Rylance play on Broadway recently. I had to get there. The Second Coming phenomenon, the promise of a religious experience. Naturally it was sold out. Unlike my mother, I did not gamble on my charm to secure a ticket. Instead, I called a friend whose sole job is to acquire house seats for a particular client and who, in emergencies, has offered his services to me. He got me a seat. That's what you have to do when you don't have quite as much of your original sparkling of charm dust, or when you have spent the sparkle elsewhere. You go to New York, you have your remarkable experience in the theater, you are sublimely happy, but you come home without having encountered the white knight. You return without a story that you whip into a winning confection, a story that will radiate into your future. It is the radiant life that perhaps keeps a person going and still going, no exercise necessary.

# Around the Table

LAUREN GRODSTEIN

Although I'm probably misremembering, I look back on my childhood mornings as periods of almost religious calm. Really, this couldn't have been the case: I was the oldest of three, so there must have been clattering dishes and missing gloves and the rest of it. But in my memory, mornings were sunlit and tranquil: I would wake up, shower (writing my name again and again on the steamy glass), get dressed, and head downstairs for breakfast in contemplative silence. My dad was already at work; my siblings were—somewhere. I'd pull out the cereal, find an old magazine, note the time on the microwave and that there were twelve or so minutes until I had to leave for school. I'd read an article in *Newsweek* or *Gourmet* about Bill Clinton or Japanese food while shoveling Cheerios into my mouth.

Then my mother would appear, pull open the freezer, and stare into it, perplexed, for up to a full minute. I'd keep my face in the magazine, steeling myself for the question I knew was coming.

"So"—in her most ruminative voice, the same voice every time—"so what should I defrost for dinner?"

Every single morning, this question, and every single morning it made me crazy. First, I had no idea what was available in the freezer; second, the very concept of "defrosting" was opaque. Third, and most important, dinner was so far away as to belong to a different dimension, somewhere beyond math, social studies, a welter of mean girls, gym class, homework, and whatever was on TV that afternoon. How could I care about something

139

that belonged so deep in the future? Anyway, wouldn't it probably just be chicken?

But even if it was just chicken, my mom had to make dinner. For our house wasn't a takeout house, wasn't a let's-just-order-a-pizza-tonight house, wasn't a boxed-mac-and-cheese or even a spaghetti-with-tomato-sauce kind of house. We were, instead, a three-course-meal kind of house, and the centerpiece, every night, was some variety of meat, paired with a vegetable and a starch, preceded by soup or a salad, followed up by ice cream for dessert, or a cookie, or if life was good, both.

The food itself was always tasty—my mom was, and is, quite a good cook, specializing in homey soups and elegant baked goods. She can take an onion and a bag of beans and turn it into something restaurant-worthy; her apple cake is the reason I still make it through the High Holidays. Whatever she did with that chicken was always yummy, and sometimes even—when there was parmesan and breadcrumbs involved—magical.

Yet no matter how good the food was, dinner itself was a chore. We had to wait to eat till my dad came home, and then he (or me, or my sister) was usually somewhat stressed out, or else my brother, who was nine years younger than me and terrible at just sitting, was wriggling out of his seat, and it was eight o'clock at night and we were somehow only up to *salad*. And even if everyone was basically calm and happy, there was still the incessant questioning: What did I do today? What happened at school? What did my sister do that day? Why weren't we eating our salad?

Someone (my sister) would try to disguise the fact that she didn't like whatever was on her plate. Someone (my brother) would start eating with his hands. Someone (me) would wish, just once, we could order pizza and eat it in front of the TV like every other family I knew. Why couldn't we ever be like everyone else? What other family on earth did this to themselves every single night?

But then again, after dinner, there was dessert.

Where this mealtime habit came from, I'm really not sure. I know that neither of my parents grew up in what we might today call foodie households;

my father's mother was a wonderful cook, but also a strict traditionalist of the noodle kugel and blintz variety.

And while I remember my maternal grandmother as a maestro of brisket and a deft assembler of cinnamon toast, my mother says that, actually, she was indifferent in the kitchen, put off by the ceaselessness of feeding her hungry family. When my grandfather retired, she announced that, unless the kids were visiting, she was no longer going to cook, which meant they survived for many years on South Florida early bird specials and Publix rotisserie chickens. They were none the worse off for it.

Nevertheless, together my parents created a household culture that valued time at the table, interesting food, and in-depth conversation. Today, if you ask them where these ideas about dinner came from, they'll both say they don't know—it certainly wasn't something they'd planned. They were not big believers in parental philosophies, so I know they weren't trying out some family-dinner-breeds-confident-kids nonsense. Nor do I think it was about the era; the meals we ate were not particularly nineties meals (I don't remember a single sun-dried tomato, for instance, nor sushi nor poppy seed vinaigrettes). My parents traveled a bit before we came along, and probably found certain inspiration in Europe, but my dad will cheerfully remember how he had no idea what escargot were during their honeymoon in France, and how the idea of drinking wine while eating cheese sounded like some kind of joke. So they weren't mimicking someone else's idea of what dinner should be, or trying to live like people they weren't.

I suppose in the end they did it because, basically, they liked the doing: they liked the sitting down and talking, they liked the good food, and no matter our fussing, they liked having us all in one place for what was (I now can see) at most thirty minutes every night. They liked it enough that it was worth the hassle of the daily defrost and the washing up; they had three small kids and busy lives, and daily pleasure was not something to take for granted. So they consciously built in the rather grand daily pleasure of a good family meal.

Twenty-five years later, they are still like this: dinner at my parents' house continues to be at least a three-course affair, and sometimes, if my dad has made time to go to the cheese section at Fairway, there's a course number four. As they've gotten older and traveled more, they've branched into more exotic fare: my dad makes ceviche, and my mom grinds her own hummus. The turkey at Thanksgiving is always wet-brined and air-dried, then given a turn in the enormous metal smoker on their deck. And now that we are all of age, there are martinis before dinner and sometimes brandy afterward, which means when I stagger upstairs to my childhood bedroom I'm often a tiny bit drunk.

Of course there are other, more important differences. For instance, we are no longer a fivesome, since all three of us children are married, with one son and one daughter apiece. It is impossible to reconstitute the five we once were amid this sprawling family: I cannot look at my brother now without seeing his lookalike daughter; I cannot imagine my sister without her husband of a decade and a half (she married young). We were a team of five, and now we are a team of fourteen.

Which means that family dinner was a time in my life that meant a thing that it will never, precisely, mean again: a mother and a father at either side of the table, a sister and a brother across from me, the anxieties of being a teenager that I would never talk about, the anxieties of being parents they would never bring up. Three courses. Clearing the table. And in the morning, once again, wondering what on earth to defrost.

And now I'm the mother.

Mornings at my own house are still generally quiet, although I'm partial to the kitchen transistor tuned to NPR when the news is tolerable. I wake up around 6:30, skip the shower, stagger downstairs to put on coffee. Ben, my husband, is already on his way to work. The kids are asleep. In the winter, the sun is starting to rise; in the summer, the light through the kitchen window is marking a spot on the floor for the dog to take her early morning nap. I make the lunches (PBJ for my son; yogurt and veggie bites for my daughter). I eat a grapefruit or some granola. After they go to school, before I go to work, I spare a minute to think about dinner.

We are, sometimes, a takeout family, and sometimes we're a mac-and-cheese-from-a-box family. But much more than I ever would have supposed, we're a sit-down-together-for-dinner family, even though my daughter is still a toddler and can't sit still for more than twenty minutes, and my nine-year-old son would be just as happy (much more happy, actually) to eat pizza in front of the TV.

We don't do courses, and if Ben is working super late, we don't wait for him to come home to eat. And because both kids are picky, I find myself making separate bowls of pasta for them sometimes, which is something my parents would *never* have done. But last night, for instance, I roasted butternut squash (cut up already at Trader Joe's) and sautéed onions and lentils. The house smelled good; my son expressed interest. After about twenty minutes, I pushed the squash to the side of the baking pan and added a few sausages (I believe this is what the food section calls a sheet-pan supper). Then, after the oven timer buzzed, I added the squash and sausages to the lentils, set the table, made my son pour us all ice water, and sat down with my family to interrogate them about their days and watch my son pretend to like butternut squash.

Twenty minutes later, we were clearing the table. Ten minutes after that, we were dishing out ice cream. And twenty years from now, my kids, I hope, will feed families of their own, and remember how it was done when they were young, and feel moved to do it themselves in their own way. There is remarkable consistency in the grand pleasure of sitting with people you love around the table.

But I'd be lying if I didn't say I sometimes miss the old team, and that time in my life when what to make for dinner was someone else's problem, and my only responsibility was eating it. I suppose there's a pleasure in that wistfulness too—in remembering the way something was and holding tight to what will also one day be a memory.

# This Truth about Chaos

JOHN FREEMAN

If my father smelled of anything through my childhood, it was cut grass and sawdust. Most evenings, before dinner, I'd find him in the garage, standing in shirtsleeves before a table covered in screws and greasy rivets, wrestling with a machine. A lawnmower, a sprinkler head, some piece of pipe. If an appliance broke, he fixed it, and if it wasn't broken, he made sure it would be by tinkering with it. My father wasn't particularly handy, but he grew up in a generation that distrusted objects they couldn't master. When these things resisted him, he'd let loose a string of compound epithets and I knew it was time to lay low.

Even then, in my early teens, I understood his fiddling with tools was a displacement activity. By day my father ran a nonprofit family service agency that provided what the government no longer would. The agency employed social workers to counsel people going on or off welfare, drivers to deliver meals to shut-in seniors, patient and skilled therapists to operate a suicide hotline at its Sacramento offices. It was good work, and I know my father was proud of it, but I also sensed—from being around him—the job was like bailing a leaky boat. One day he arrived home flecked in blood: a client had cut her arms open and died in the office entryway.

The state didn't fund these services, and so part of my father's job involved scrounging five- and six-figure checks from the very people who'd voted to undo the government safety net that once protected the poor and indigent. Occasionally, my two brothers and I were roped in to work the coat check at his fund-raisers. We'd put on our blue blazers with brass buttons and accept folded dollar bills to watch over the belongings of wealthy Californians who paid $250 for a dinner to benefit a good cause—a fraction of a fraction of what they'd probably received from trickle-down tax breaks. On one of these nights, I was amazed at how a few hours' worth of tips filled my pocket fatter than a month of delivering newspapers. Then I realized that was exactly what my father was probably thinking in that room, shaking hands, smiling with gritted teeth. Their financial dandruff would keep his operation running.

This position of dependence made my father irate. It seemed obvious to him that if you had enough, you gave some away; if you had a lot, then the size of your giving should follow. But we were living through a time that has reached perhaps its apogee now, of defining poverty as a choice and mental health problems as weakness and government intervention as a form of idiocy beyond words. One night in the middle of a heavy grant-writing period, my father nearly turned the dining table over with frustration. "What if I tell them *we help burned children*?" he yelled at my mother, who, as usual, was trying to talk him down. "Do you think that'd be enough? We help *burned* children."

My father almost didn't become this person: the class warrior who rejected a silver spoon for a life of social work. Growing up he'd been a class clown and mama's boy who played football and drove a brand new Chevy v8. His family lived in the Fabulous Forties, a Sacramento neighborhood made famous by the film *Lady Bird*. Governor Reagan was a neighbor; my grandfather, raised in San Francisco after the earthquake fire, was in the Gipper's cabinet. Meantime, my father drank and partied and very nearly didn't even get into community college. It was by the skin of his teeth that he'd later manage to transfer into Berkeley, where his father had paid his own way during the Depression, and after graduation my father was so lost he briefly worked as a prison guard before he joined the seminary. Which he then dropped out of after he read Nietzsche. I don't know how he found social work, but he did, and eventually, in his middle thirties, realized it was what he was meant for.

As counselors, my parents both worked in a form of narrative therapy—people told stories to them to sort out who they were and why they were so troubled. Similarly, my parents told their own stories back to us—in particular, my father's. Oddly, it was my mother imparting my father's origin story most often, not him. At night, if he lost his temper, she'd slip into my room on tiptoes and explain how badly my father didn't want us to live the same way he had—zigzagging, emotionally neglected. That and work were why he was so tense.

I didn't for a second doubt her, nor do I now. I know my father loves us; I am lucky to have him in my life and to believe this with all my heart. My father's approach to fathering, though, was to flood the zone, to borrow a phrase from old *New York Times* editor Howell Raines, whose philosophy on big news stories was, Why do one piece when you could assign six? No activity I participated in growing up went unchecked, unsupervised, or untested for nutritional value. If I appeared to have free time, my father would dig up a reading list from a school district *back east*, as the East Coast was called. Or I'd be dispatched to earn a Boy Scout merit badge so rarely pursued it even stumped the scout master. *Huh, they have architecture?* By the age of thirteen, stoked by my father's horror stories of the career-less and dissolute—*you want to be driving a Subaru and watching Sacramento Kings games your whole life?!*—I'd interned in several possible careers—medicine, architecture, and even law—and found them wanting.

In essence, my father treated us as if we were being homeschooled, even though we attended school for ten hours of the day. It was a luxury to have such care, but also a burden, because it is in the nature of adolescents to be fickle and lazy, to discard interests like snakeskin and find new things. We did all of this, and it incensed my father. He was so desperate for us to succeed as adults he treated us like adults, explaining what could go wrong at adult levels—*do you want to wind up in prison, maybe you start drinking, and then what, you accidentally hit someone driving home at night?*—even giving us condoms at age ten. I socked mine away until they rotted; my older brother eventually used his; my little brother turned his into water balloons and threw them at passing cars.

My father had a weird and unexpected sense of humor in those days, but not about failure. Growing up in the shadow of his love, we felt like failures waiting to happen. This wasn't misinterpretation because he often used those very words. Listening through the wall one night as he tried to help my older brother complete his math homework, I heard my father shout over and over each time Andy offered up the incorrect answer. "Wrong! You're a failure! You're a failure! Just give up!" And then I heard my father storm out of the room, slamming the door, making the house shake.

The zoom and swerve of my father's anger was the weather system of those years, and it was frankly terrifying. A conversation often escalated from questions across some unseen thermal to tornadic interrogation so fast it was bewildering. He wasn't a tall man, but he was *dense* and phenomenally strong, and we came to know this. My father once caught my older brother and me wrestling in our front yard, and a split second after I saw his shoe in my peripheral vision, we were airborne. He'd flung both of us into the bushes as if we were lightly packed duffel bags. It got worse, and it was unpleasant, and I spent a lot of my early teens in a constant state of fear.

My older brother bore the brunt of this fury; my younger brother took on a posture of the victim; my response was to become very, very independent. I took on after-school activities and rarely turned up at home before seven. I became a reader so my mind was literally elsewhere. Playing six sports a year, I sculpted my body into a defensive weapon. I didn't get into fights, but people would have to think twice before pushing me around. Including him. The result of these strategies was that I developed a sense of double-ness that has become permanent over time. Like I watch everything happen in front of me a moment before it actually happens and then dispatch the person playing me to handle it.

For this reason, I have come to feel at home around volatile people. Around those who demand a lot and create the mood, who make decisions and set terms. It's familiar. I don't even need to deploy this doubleness; it just happens. Whenever I felt the ground shift, when I knew my father was at the edge's edge, I learned how to deflect and anticipate; I figured out when to disappear. I did this so well I became a seismologist of mood and could even predict the tremors before they happened. And so now, as a forty-four-year-old, when a fault line slips in virtually any situation, I am already halfway there to meet it. I have already begun booting up a whole variety of de-escalation strategies—conversational, nonverbal, physical. In other words, without realizing it, my father spent a lot of my teenage years molding me perfectly into the shape of a receptive editor.

Someone who could adapt to a wide variety of intensities and insanities.

As I writer, I say this with affection and knowledge of my own insanities. We are terrible people sometimes, writers. Narcissistic, belligerent, single-minded, and strange. The rising forms of mania that accompany peculiarly small details are endless. I understand why. Writers are in control of their work and nothing else. And yet their survival often depends heavily on that *nothing else*. Getting reviews or teaching jobs or book sales over which they have often very little control. This is a recipe for intense anxiety. Even if you discount the attendant worries about whether work will last, if it is in fact any good, people also have to eat, they need health care (in America), they need roofs over their heads and school for their children, if they have them. Providing any significant part of this on a writer's salary is virtually impossible. It's ludicrous. Even Zadie Smith and Jhumpa Lahiri teach—what does that tell you? Given the influence of reputations on grants and awards, this bind of dependency is ever more stressful.

I knew early on, watching my father work, and sitting next to my mother as she took down notes from patients dying of Parkinson's and AIDS, that I didn't have it in me to be on the front line of care for others. My mother spent most of my teenager years driving upward of 150 miles a day to remote houses to counsel people about to lose a loved one about what they were facing. It was grim and important and grinding work, and you needed more than belief to do it—you needed a temperament of patience and something else, something almost holy, I hesitate to say, to do it. I thought about this a lot when my mother too eventually fell ill, and then got worse, and finally became the kind of patient someone like her—a social worker in a car—came to visit. They were mostly there to talk to my dad, to see how he was doing, holding what must have felt like the earth on his shoulders all day. On the day she died, my father sent the social worker away. It was as if he knew right away that the next weight he would have to lift would be her absence. At first he'd want to do that alone.

I wished I had this temperament. I loved my mother dearly and admired her even more than my father for the way she contained all those terrible stories and made people feel better. When I became a writer, it didn't even occur to me to make a story up: she was living proof it wasn't necessary. They were all around us, eating away at people's bodies. My father may have been the bully sometimes, but my mother is the one who taught me the hardest lesson. In hearing about just a few of her cases, it was clear to me that chaos was out there, waiting for all of us in some form or other. Usually lying in wait in our bodies. In the end, it would catch us. My father pressed down hard, sometimes too hard, thinking he'd protect us from this truth about chaos, and in so doing he made me into someone who would try to help those with a rage to shape it.

I made this connection not long ago. I was in Sacramento visiting my father. He lives there today with his second wife in the old neighborhood where he grew up, driving a car he would have made fun of back in my teenage years, and doing a lot of beautiful gardening, some volunteer work—like escorting women to clinics that provide abortions—and vigorous walking. One of the bewildering changes for me about his life since he remarried has been a shift in his domestic sphere. The home I grew up in was terrific but in a constant state of disarray. The house my father now lives in and its gardens could be a museum.

Pulling into it late one night on a visit, I was so confused as to doubt I'd reached the right address. Sitting there, engine idling, it brought me back to the late 1980s and early 1990s, when no matter how hard I tried to avoid the house I lived in, I was beholden to it on the weekends.

Even when I had an away game or track meet, I had to spend thirty-six or more hours in our house. Living in the Central Valley meant you could plant, mow, prune, trim, and generally molest your yard for ten or eleven months out of the year. On weekends my father set to our lawns with a rage that was almost comical. One summer he ripped out the ivy in our palm tree one leaf at a time. Another summer he dug a sunken garden and planted eucalyptus trees so the pet rabbit we'd lost interest in had somewhere cool to graze. Every week she dug six feet down beneath the fence pilings and tunneled to freedom.

Every single task we performed in the yard was rapidly, hilariously undone by nature. Foxes ate grapes off the vine we planted. Raccoons nibbled the flower buds. The lawn browned in the baking sun just as fast as you watered it, and trying to get around sprinkler laws with slow-rotating backyard water dispersal units was dangerous. One Sunday morning I was woken by my father screaming in the kitchen—the thing had rolled over and nearly severed one of his gnarled ex-tight-end fingers.

I wish my mother were still here to fill me in on her version of this period of our lives together. She was the one who prized my father's fore-finger from the jaws of death, and I think she also told him he had to stop hitting us. Because at some point in this time it ceased—and more and more often she'd shake me from a dream on a weekend morning, her face twisted in uncharacteristic anger, and yell at me to *go out there and help your father, he's fifty years old, he'll have a heart attack*.

So I'd lope out to the yard and find my father with his back to the house. Tending the sunflowers or clipping weeds, laying down mulch for the rhododendrons. Sometimes he'd give me something to do, but as I got older, he'd send me away or I'd have to force him to let me help. I think he just wanted to be alone. Sometimes, we'd drive off to the nursery to buy fertilizer for the azaleas or some new flower he'd nestle in against one of the fences. By dusk he'd be sunburned and salt-streaked and very, very quiet. After dinner, as we watched the evening news or a basketball game, he'd ask my brothers and me for backrubs. He had a huge back, and it took all three of us.

# No Indifferent Place

CAROLYN FERRELL

Summer 1968: two six-year-old girls, a hot Long Island afternoon, wheez-
ing refrigerator and suburban kitchen papered in golden burlap and
floral trim, beige linoleum peeling at the edges of the floor. Stacy Brown
looking at me funny. Because we lived next door to each other in a so-
called colored development of tepid Cape Cods, my kitchen looked just
like Stacy's. Except for the shallow bowl of curdled milk on the counter.
"You gonna eat that?" she asked. Grimacing, I took a spoonful, and then
another. Her eyes never left my mouth.

I made a face, but in fact I loved *Dickmilch*. If you put enough sugar on
top, you could spoon it into your mouth thinking you were eating yogurt
(supermarket yogurt was too expensive, my mother explained in the aisles
of Hills). For Stacy's sake I feigned gagging, crossed my eyes, screwed
up my nose; this was not the first time I playacted for one of the kids on
our block; it would not be the last time I made fun of our odd ways in
order to hear North Ronald Drive laugh. There were the obvious flaws:
We had no plastic slipcovers, we didn't play James Brown records on our
stereo, we were a family led by a white woman married to a black man
living in a black neighborhood, and we went around like it was nothing
weird. I was forever at the ready with a quip when someone looked at us
strangely: "It's because we're half German," I'd explain in an all-knowing
way. Half-German meant *cultured*, it meant *excusably* weird: That's how
they did things in Europe (a place where rich and famous people went
on vacations). A girl down the street once complained that I gave myself

airs, but those airs were my armor. When I wasn't feeling ashamed or bewildered, I fancied our difference as a badge of honor. When I was in junior high, a well-meaning relative gave me a comic book titled *How to Be a Nonconformist*.

"I wouldn't eat that if you paid me," Stacy Brown said after watching me down the last of the *Dickmilch*. She went home. I envisioned Stacy's mother, Henrietta, taking the arm of a neighbor and whispering in her ear at the chain-link fence.

*Hey Girl, you wanna hear something? Elke Ferrell be giving her kids spoiled milk to eat.*

*You lying!*

*As God is my witness!*

*Can't they afford yogurt? It's always on sale.*

*Me, I don't go in for that sort of thing.*

*What thing?*

*White people's food.*

*Oh, yeah. Me neither.*

I wanted to run after Stacy and tell her I was *on her side*; different, yes, and yet just like her. Because just like her, I used the word *ain't* (never within my mother's earshot—as an immigrant, she prized correct grammar), and like Stacy, I looked askance at the misdeeds and quirks of white people, who could be mean, unpredictable, and (as my babysitter CeCe once explained) *prejudiced*. They were the worst definition, in other words, of weird. They shouldn't have to be accepted. I wondered where my own mother fit in this confusion of laws. She was mostly no-nonsense. She hated all prejudice—one reason she had to leave Germany was that the postwar air was filled with the dregs of Nazi sentiment, of what the Germans had "lost." My mother found that untenable. She despised the way her father nostalgically admired German soldiers, "the best on earth" in his words, while he gambled away their finances and she went hungry. She saw nothing wrong in dating a black GI and turned her back on the brother who subsequently pronounced her "dead to him." As a child I recognized a certain decency, a humanity, absent from all the weird and evil white people I knew—whom our block knew—were roaming the earth.

My mother's mother fell into this last category. During Mutti's infrequent visits to Long Island, my mother's demeanor ran the rainbow from joy to misery. Mutti refused to learn English; she criticized my mother for not teaching her children German; she was overbearing, domineering. This was the woman who'd spurned her daughter after she left to be with a black man in America. The woman who declared that any children my mother might have with said black man would never be recognized by her *real* family. On one visit, Mutti took a late afternoon walk and didn't return for hours. Eventually she was escorted home safely by a stranger, a black man who understood, despite the language barrier, that she was lost. When my mother called my father to deliver the good news, he said he wished she would've stayed lost forever.

My mother chose to live as a stranger in a strange land; years later, I found myself in similar circumstances. I traveled to Germany after graduating college, to study literature at the Free University in Berlin. The experience was cold, lonely, and also captivating—I found a copy of Rilke's *Letters to a Young Poet* in a thrift shop in Kreuzberg and read and reread each page religiously. In one letter from 1903, Rilke advises aspiring young poet (and seemingly overall melancholic) Franz Kappus to look to his own experience for inspiration, not turn from it. If Kappus was unable to find subject matter there, well, then maybe he wasn't cut out for the gritty life of a writer. "If your everyday life seems poor," Rilke writes, "don't blame it; blame yourself; admit to yourself that you are not enough of a poet to call forth its riches; because for the creator there is no poverty and no indifferent place. And even if you found yourself in some prison, whose walls let in none of the world's sounds—wouldn't you still have your childhood, that jewel beyond all price, that treasure house of memories?" I (practicing my own melancholia) figured I was not the first lonely student to pick up the volume and identify with it *too much*. But the book became a life raft. I had my official reason for being in an occupied city—I was a student on a grant—but perhaps there was a hidden reason (besides an idiotic heartthrob, Ekkehard, whom I'd followed to West Berlin, stupidly in love). Perhaps I stayed in that unforgiving, coldhearted city because it was like the town I'd grown up in, my mother's first refuge from postwar Germany. Perhaps there is a sentimental impulse to think these harsh places address the dearth we find within ourselves, that encountering the difficult is necessary for our growth. In a sense, my mother and I both had run away, although we went through "proper channels" to do so. But something fueled us, and Rilke's words urged me to look back, to gather, to learn from the footsteps I'd already taken. To take in my mother's footsteps and hold them deep inside. "You must realize that something is happening to you, that life has not forgotten you, that it holds you in its hand and will not let you fall." Rilke's letters instructed me to grow, and I felt his words sink slowly into my bones, even if my brain and heart were not yet able to cooperate.

When I was six, seven, eight, and older, my circumstances seemed to guarantee a lifetime of misery: a poverty of experience, of financial hardship, and sadly, of love. I longed for escape. College, a husband, a nice house—as a kid I fantasized actually climbing into someone's *Mystery Date* game and finding there a hidden brown man for me. Maybe it was also, though, a foreknowledge of my grandparents' racism that helped me cast the first stones at my complicated family, and that paved the way for my eventual self-exile. I loved to make people laugh and, in this way, knew I could both point out my weirdness and be applauded for it at the same time. When I was in the third grade, my mother made me sardines in tomato sauce on rye bread for lunch; I laughed loudest when the other kids moved to a different table with their hamburgers and fish sticks. In junior high school, when my friends gave themselves cool nicknames, I tried to get them to call me *Schaetzchen*, my mother's version of "Sweetie." No one did. I had nothing to say (but some shame to feel) when my mother dressed us in bathing suits and allowed us to dance on the front lawn during rainstorms, even as, down the street, the church services that normal black people attended, were about to start.

My parents didn't seem to care what the block felt about them, and my mother, overworked with four kids and an endless flow of neighborhood toddlers she babysat on afternoons and weekends, often didn't notice what I was going through. She was too busy to see how I was bullied by children of the street and by my own father. She survived by adapting to American life, to black life, to the severity of my father. From him she received a meager ten-dollar weekly allowance for food and clothes; she was expected to put his breakfast on the table every morning at four—even the day after she arrived home from the hospital with their fourth child. *You're my wife, and that's your job.* I often dreamt of them separating and remember feeling something like glee when I discovered the concept of divorce. Once when she took us for the summer to see her parents in northern Germany, he followed a few weeks later, perhaps fearing she wouldn't come back. When he arrived, I remember feeling my heart jump, but once we returned to the United States, things fell back into miserable place. Laundry, babies, cooking, cleaning, loneliness. Amid it all, I watched my mother's strength and bitterness and hope and desolation taking turns in bloom and shadow. During a visit from Hamburg, my mother's sister didn't hold back from commenting on how poor our life seemed—she wanted my mother to return to Germany, to a happy life she believed was only possible over there. No, my mother said. Her home was here.

And home was not always bad. Moments of light slipped through when you weren't looking: When I was seven years old, my father built a three-foot-deep pool in our backyard (next to a wooden playhouse he built for my birthday and wooden lawn furniture he built for my mother). The pool was thinly corrugated aluminum so frail one wrong kick would knock it over. Nevertheless, my mother swam in it every day, even as we kids thrashed about. No one else on the block had a pool, even one as makeshift as this. Later my father would install a sturdier pool and monkey bars alongside so we could swing ourselves into the water. My father had never learned to swim; perhaps that was why he set up the flimsy pool—she wouldn't have the opportunity to swim away. Not across the Great South Bay, not across the ocean. Occasionally a neighbor woman would look over the fence, eyebrows raised, the balloon above her head reading: *What is this grown woman doing in this kiddie pool?* My mother would say something like, "It's so hot, isn't it?" Even though nothing had actually been asked.

People did not always balk at my mother's difference; some looked past it to see her warmth and generosity. Neighbors left their children with her: At times she had more than eight kids a day, playing at our pool table in the basement, or outside on the swings, or with our toys in our rooms. There were afternoons of great happiness, and yet the voice of our German grandmother flowed from the reel-to-reel tapes in the living room straight into our dreams at night: *Why don't you come home?*

North Ronald Drive was a Kafkaesque fever dream. I spent a lot of time running—from bullies, from kids who hated my hair and skin, and from my father, who turned his everyday misanthropy on all around him. I hid in bushes, faked stomach aches to leave school, and threw my diary across the room when it didn't protect me. We lived there until my father decided we should start anew in California—my parents' marriage was shattering, and the mythical West promised salvation. My neighborhood had never made much sense to me, but I wasn't ready for any other fever dream than the one on Long Island.

In West Berlin, I found myself crying often. It was the winter of 1985, and though I'd tenaciously planted myself there two months earlier, I had no friends. I lived in an unheated apartment, and my meager student loan left me broke by the middle of each month. Ekkehard, man of my dreams, told me I should commit myself to a mental asylum. Day in and day out I was on the phone with my mother (a tough thing, given the cost), and homesickness was about to do me in. "Should I come back New York?" I asked. I hated West Berlin and its grimy, xenophobic residents. I had been forced to move a few times, and when I went looking for a room to rent, people often slammed the door in my face saying, "KEINE AUSLÄNDER!"

My relatives—when I visited them in the West—belittled my concerns about the racism I encountered. Why did I want to study in Germany if it was so bad? they asked. Had my American education been so lacking? Don't feel bad about the color of your skin, one said to me—but had I ever expressed such a feeling? Once, while visiting my uncle in his small village outside Kiel, I took a walk in the forest and was accosted by an elfin elderly man. "I know where you're from!" he shouted. "Africa!" Another time, a relative I hadn't seen in years greeted me at her door with an apron and a bucket of soapy water. "Hilfst Du mir beim Fensterputzen?" she asked. I wasn't there to clean her windows, I explained. Just to visit.

I yearned for my mother's love. Sitting in my gray Neukoelln apartment one frigid day, bawling on the overseas line, what I really wanted was for her to drop everything and come to me. I wanted her to realize how much she missed Germany—even if gritty West Berlin was not like the northern Germany of her youth. On some level I was in Germany living the life she should have had—a university experience, the chance to travel Europe. Payback for all those hard years on Long Island. "Don't you want to come back home one day?" I asked, sniffling into the receiver. But I knew the answer without her having to say a word. She'd been in the United States for more than forty years. Four kids, a messy divorce, no child support—in spite of this, my mother loved the life America had given her. She loved her independence. She loved being around different kinds of people and not breathing in a Nazi past. My father had once been her escape; at the start of their marriage, he was kind and often considerate. But the marriage failed, and my mother literally escaped California to return to New York, to the same Long Island village (albeit in a different neighborhood). She put us back in our old schools and made as if this little California blip never happened.

She went on to find my stepfather, a man whose interests matched hers and whose love for her grew peacefully and whole. She put her kids through college and then, at seventy, got her own bachelor's degree. Sure, she'd kept Germany in her heart—one of her favorite pastimes is still a walk on the beach, preferably at Fire Island, a place reminiscent of the

Baltic seacoast where she'd grown up. Her mother made her and her sisters bathe in the sea each morning before school—to build character. There was always a smell of climbing roses in the air and fresh bread wafting from Mutti's kitchen. But that Germany was gone.

"I love my life here," she said to me, just a few years ago. "I don't want to go back."

What took me so long to get the message? And why hadn't I realized that this message was her gift to me?

"Your mom left that bowl of milk out on the counter all morning?"

"Yes."

"You gonna get sick. You all crazy."

I remember buying a supermarket container of *Dickmilch* in Berlin and wondering why my mother hadn't at least put fruit at the bottom of hers. This stuff was actually pretty great with fruit.

On North Ronald Drive, Olive Bean lived two doors down and worked for the New York City Board of Education. She loved my mother. Olive's daughter, CeCe, would come over after school and babysit me. I idolized her from the start. I knew books were a big deal in their house, as was the large drawing of Angela Davis that sat on an easel in their living room. Once, CeCe brought over a copy of *Harriet the Spy* and placed it in my hands. I felt my heart race when it was over. How astonishing: A girl who actually took notes of her own observations and thoughts and had the gumption to consider herself a writer.

When I was six and my sister five, we got into a fight: Who was going to get to be an artist when she grew up? My mother, pregnant with my second brother, put aside her broom and took us by the arms. Dinner was on the stove; dirty diapers floated in the toilet. "You can be the artist," she said to my sister. And turning to me: "You can be the writer."

"Listen to me," my mother urged on the phone. I couldn't stop crying. "Listen to me. You have to decide whether to stay and make the most of this opportunity. Or else you have to come home. You have to make a decision." I looked at the coal oven in the corner of my West Berlin studio, the oven that hadn't worked in weeks, and then I looked at my cat, who sat atop a ladder in order to stay warm. "It took me fifteen years to grow up," she said. "You have to do it right now."

I thought back to high school, a particularly difficult time. After California, my mother moved us into a crumbly Cape on the dividing line of our racially divided village and began working four jobs to pay our bills. I was free from the chains of the authoritarian household that had once contained my father, but ill-equipped to handle that freedom. Though our life together had been fraught, I missed my family as a unit; my self-esteem suffered. Boyfriends in high school ranged from indifferent to abusive. I felt teachers lose faith in me; my guidance counselor advised me to apply to community college, because, he asked, "Why do you think a place like Sarah Lawrence College will accept *you* for admission?" But what was the alternative?

At Sarah Lawrence, in one writing workshop after another, I learned that the horrible, wonderful treasures of my childhood were just that: jewels. I would always have to eat that spoiled milk. I would always have to wish for that James Brown record to play in our house. My church was not a brick building wherein Easter coats and satin sashes announced the pinnacle of girldom—solid *black* girldom, without any trace of whiteness. That was not me. My church was my hand around a pencil, my fingers on a word-processing keyboard. "Do you suppose that someone who really has [God] could lose him like a little stone?" Rilke asked before answering his own question. "We must trust in what is difficult."

I hung up the phone. Without my knowing it, the puzzle pieces began to clunk into place. Our lives ran parallel courses, the inheritance of both strength and fear, the negotiation of yearning and impermanence, the jigsaw that was emerging and would emerge for the rest of my life. Her life.

"There is only one solitude," Rilke writes in another letter, "and it is vast, heavy, difficult to bear, and almost everyone has hours when he would gladly exchange it for any kind of sociability, however trivial. . . .

But perhaps these are the very hours during which solitude grows; for its growing is painful as the growing of boys and sad as the beginning of spring." The solitude of my childhood was informing my life in West Berlin; I was becoming the writer I needed to become. The writer my mother wanted me to become.

I stayed in Europe for three years, and during university breaks, I occasionally found myself at Mutti's house in Schleswig Holstein. We would sit in her garden, where she narrated her life as if it were a movie. She never spoke of calling the military police on my father the first time he visited their home in 1960. She said she never knew what was happening to the Jews during the war—no one did, she claimed—and she feigned ignorance when I discovered in her linen closet a tablecloth embroidered with swastikas. In her bedroom, my grandmother kept a painted chest full of handcrafted books she'd filled over the years with stories and poems. Some true. Some so full of yearning it hurt to hear her read them. My grandmother's little books were her treasures. I leafed through them, holding those miniature volumes in my hands, perhaps in prayer. I didn't want my stories to end up hidden in a pretty chest. Back in West Berlin, I began to make friends. I walked the city, went to the opera, to films, to plays. I moved in with kind people. I played violin in an orchestra; I played chamber music with friends. I wrote my mother about my emerging life in Germany, and she wrote back, full of admiration and happiness and hope. She told her friends about the things I did—they were all nurses like her, working the overnight shift—and they cheered me on from the ICU.

Eventually, I came back to New York and worked on my short stories, many of which took me back to that block on Long Island and that bowl of sour milk. "You mustn't be frightened, dear Mr. Kappus," Rilke wrote in 1904, "if a sadness rises in front of you, larger than any you have ever seen . . . you must realize that something is happening to you, that life has not forgotten you, that it holds you in its hand and will not let you fall. Why do you want to shut out of your life any uneasiness, any misery, any depression, since after all you don't know what work these conditions are doing inside you?" This was the best writerly advice I could have gotten as I sat in West Berlin, devising ways for my mother to return and knowing she wouldn't. She *couldn't*. "In you so much is happening now," Rilke went on, "you must be patient like someone who is sick, and confident like someone who is recovering, for perhaps you are both."

That was not me, I remember thinking. But of course, it was me all along.

# And Niriko Makes Four

LOLIS ERIC ELIE

There's something I wanted to tell you, wish I could have told you in those last few days when you hovered at the crossroads between this world and that: You have a grandson. Lolis Niriko.

He wasn't born then. Indeed he had been scarcely imagined. I had met his mother already, but only through phone and email.

You never said you wanted grandchildren. Was it irony or poetic justice that led your granddaughter, Tyese—the child of the child you fathered before you met my mother—from Harlem to your doorstep several months into your dotage? In your more lucid moments, you could remember who she was and brag to friends about the impressive young woman in the new picture on your mantel. But those moments were spacing themselves further and further apart. I told Tye that, had she come even a year earlier, you would have feted her like the biblical father feted his prodigal son. You would have shown her off at Upperline and Commander's Palace and Dooky Chase and popped bottles of Champagne until everyone had drunk their fill.

Or were you the prodigal, having absented yourself from her late mother's life so many years before?

Be that as it may, coming when she did, she got only the ghost of her grandfather and the photos and videos I have since sent. My son is too late even for that.

Béa, Lolis Niriko's mother, is from Madagascar. Your grandson is Malagasy. Born of an African island about as far away from New Orleans as one can get. *The African intellectuals are superior to the black American ones*, you once said, and I took it as a kind of gospel as I was wont to do in my formative years when it seemed that, if you didn't know everything, you knew everything worth knowing. That statement, like so many of your grander pronouncements, has not held up. But statements like that led me to Africa again and again. Your politics helped shape my geography.

Vaughn Fauria—friend of yours, friend of mine, younger than you, older than me—was sometimes a bridge between us. She said that your inclination to grand statement and grandstanding had everything to do with your youth in *Niggertown*. In that small, dark corner of New Orleans, where so much of the world's knowledge and light was forbidden from crossing the color line, it must have been great sport to boast of knowing more about the world outside that world than anyone knew within it. Who among those residing there could have checked the facts? I suppose that's what empowered my grandfather, Theophile Jones Elie Sr., to tell his neighbors that he went to the World Series every year. He did wear a coat and tie when he went to his job driving a truck. I suppose somehow that counts as seeing a larger world within yourself, does it not?

An old girlfriend of mine once said that I was quick to offer my commentary, whether I was familiar with the subject matter at hand or not. When I realized she was right, I resolved that my knowledge and my words should be more directly proportional. You used to quote Gandhi, saying, "I go from truth to truth." Which is to say, "As I get more knowledge, my position may shift." I've never been able verify that Gandhi said that. It might have been original to you.

You told me a story once of your father coming to our house after church one Sunday. No doubt my mother, my sister, and I were still at our own church, Bethany United Methodist, that place you stopped attending when the congregation thought it more important to build a new sanctuary than to minister to the poor and afflicted in the nearby Desire Public Housing Development. As I recall it, you were driving along St. Charles Avenue, that grand product of cotton blood and sugar blood. Black blood. You asked your father if he had ever thought that he deserved one of those great mansions of his own. A light went off or a revelation landed or whatever it was that you said happened to him. The metaphor doesn't matter. The point is that people like us deserved mansions like those, and if we failed to attain them, it should not be for lack of belief in our own worthiness and worth.

You never doubted your worthiness, that's for sure. But your interest in saving the sons and daughters and cousins and kinfolks of the people in the Desire and Niggertown and elsewhere was always more important than amassing the money those blood mansions demanded. I remember one woman Richard Nixon accused of welfare fraud during one of his many efforts to get Watergate off the front page of the newspaper and welfare recipients onto it. You served as her lawyer for free, as if the act was striking a blow at Tricky Dick himself. You told me later that when she had a personal injury case, a case that could have actually earned a lawyer a few dollars for relatively little work, she hired a white man. By the time you told me that, it was an old story and your bitterness had faded or been buried.

Your tax trouble was a mistake of your own making, though. Your friend Leonard Dreyfuss gave you the money ($10,000 was it?) to pay the IRS debt. But by then, the white folk in nearby Hahnville had railroaded sixteen-year-old Gary Tyler to the distinction of being the youngest person on death row in Angola State Penitentiary. A white boy had been shot during school desegregation. Some black boy had to pay. You appointed yourself to the task of helping with Tyler's legal appeal, using the tax money to pay your bills. Forty years later, Gary Tyler was finally out of jail. When I met him, he thanked me for your work. By that time, you were remembering less and less.

In college, I was president of the Black Students League. If we could just commit ourselves to "the struggle," I thought—a struggle that straddled divestment from South Africa, more black faculty, more black students—we could accomplish it all. Have it all. Your optimism was my optimism. I helped lead a big movement of black students during my senior year.

If I were to have been expelled for my activity, not that it ever came anywhere near that, I was confident that I'd be welcomed home a hero. It felt good when you came to visit and heard the professors praising that work. You used to say that the family business was the shoeshine stand in Niggertown, where you learned the trade you would later ply on the streets of midtown Manhattan. Lacking the skill to blacken boots, I decided that the family business had something to do with social service.

You used to say that most of these black leaders who jump in front of the television cameras, if they were ever called to account for their stewardship, would have little to show for themselves. "Stewardship?" Perhaps you did gain something, at least a little, from all those years your mother and my mother insisted that you go to church. I always wanted to be sure that I could account for my stewardship, that wherever I was, I did my part. And I shared your impatience with those who didn't.

You loved Ralph Ellison's *Invisible Man*, especially the section when the narrator realizes that the president of his Negro college has lied to him. My favorite passage from that book concerned the college's founder: Was he lifting the veil of ignorance from the Negro or holding it more firmly in place? I inherited your contempt for those kinds of people, those people who won the praise of white people for their stewardship precisely because it was so antithetical to our interests.

You never tired of telling the story of the day we were eating lunch at Palace Café and ran into Revius Ortique. His civil rights credentials were invented and inflated, you would say. A veteran of the civil rights movement yourself, your contempt for him was palpable.

We had arrived just as he and his party were finishing their meal. You made it clear to me with that wave-of-the-hands gesture of yours that you wished he would not come over and speak to us. So of course he did. He came to our table to brag on how much business had been set aside for black contractors at the airport. I was fine for a moment.

But when he went on and on about all he had done, I could no longer be civil. I don't remember the pointed questions I asked him, but he seemed genuinely surprised that I doubted his heroism. Was that because of the things you had told me about him? Perhaps. But maybe it was because I remembered, as you never forgot, another story of black leaders claiming to help but actually hurting black business, black progress. Rhodes Limousine Service, the black-owned company, had a contract to pick up travelers at the airport. Though Ortique was not chairman of the New Orleans Aviation Board then, it was a black mayor, Dutch Morial, who stripped that contract from Rhodes and gave it to a white company. Then Morial added insult to injury by allowing that white company to raise the rates it charged. When Rhodes had made that request, they were denied.

Perhaps I should have been gentler years later when I wrote a newspaper column about the airport changing its name to honor native son Louis Armstrong. I interviewed Ortique about whether jazz musicians would benefit from this belated recognition of one of their own. Ortique, an old man by then, seemed genuinely offended at the thought of paying musicians to perform. When I pointed out that lawyers were routinely paid by the airport, he explained to me that lawyers are professionals. My reaction, as someone whose father took him to jazz clubs years before he was old enough to be legally admitted, was fiery. I wrote a scathing column that was as much a rebuke of that one man as it was a rebuke of all the "Negro" leaders who denigrated black cultural expression.

Which is to say, I have something of your hair-trigger temper. This inclination of politicians to offer me shit and tell me it's Shinola has always riled me. I sometimes wish I could control the impulse better. Then I think of the writer Christopher Hitchens, whose reaction upon being told he was a knee-jerk liberal was that he would be gravely concerned if, when faced with certain stimuli, his knee failed to jerk.

You would have said that this impulse in you came from your uncle Edward, whom you never actually knew. He and his wife raised your mother, which is why she made Edward your middle name. He was so radical, your mother told you, the priest turned his casket away at the Catholic graveyard. I'm not sure what Edward could have done in Point Coupee Parish that was bad enough to piss off that white priest (but not so bad as to get him lynched). Whatever it was, you took great pride in it. I didn't hear this story until I was grown. By then I knew that, though my first name was, like yours, Lolis, the plan was to call me by my middle name, Eric, the thirty-first most popular American boys' name in the year of my birth.

Long before my son was born, I knew that he would share our first name, the family name, but that he'd be a junior to neither of us. His middle name would be an African name, I knew. (Neither the Arabs nor the Europeans need our help in propagating their names.) "Niriko" his mother decided. It means "what I desire" in Malagasy, and it captured both our attitudes.

Béa doesn't like dogs, or at least not big ones. This I learned after renting us a room at a bed and breakfast where the owners had two large dogs and several small ones. Learning that about her made me think of you. You never liked dogs either. You swore that your father had spent far less time with you and your eight siblings than he did with his German shepherds. You were determined to exceed that low bar, and you did.

With you I discovered the joys of the Vieux Carré. There were the French Quarter walks, the potato-onion-cheese omelettes, the restaurants, the trips to Navarre Beach, that Romare Bearden exhibit at the Contemporary Arts Center. You taught me the beauty of old buildings.

You also taught me the necessity of covering tropicals when freezing weather is in the forecast. When you were growing up, your mother and sister, Mary Elizabeth and Auntie Odette, kept a rose garden in the front of the shotgun double they shared with their children. You took great pride in that. Living in Niggertown didn't have to mean living without beauty, you used to say.

You predicted that I would come to love gardens one day. This you said as we engaged in the hard winter work of moving the large collection of bromeliads that resided in the courtyard you shared with James Dombrowski, the old Communist. Watering the flowerbed was a daily job at my mother's house, often done while other kids were playing football in the street or artfully doing nothing on someone's front porch. The idea that I would voluntarily garden counted among your crazier predications. Perhaps I remembered it because of its insanity.

Insanity is well rooted in this family.

Last week, I planted coleus and canna and bird of paradise in the garden of the house I just moved into. It took me four months to actually do the work. Like you, I was not anxious to get on my hands and knees in the dirt to arrange plants and spread mulch. But like you and your mother, Mama Lizzie, and my mother and her mother, Grammy, I couldn't bear the thought of coming home to a house with little in the front yard but grass and plain, green bushes.

Then there's the story my mother tells of a day before you had left us. She wasn't feeling well, and you agreed to watch my sister and me while she took a nap. She woke to find us alone and you somewhere else. On the golf course, maybe? There was also that time after the divorce that I don't remember when my mother says my suitcase and I waited at the front door for you to pick us up. You never came.

Perhaps you and your father were not as different as you had hoped.

It must have been strange for my mother to see me becoming so much like you despite your relative absence. Was it mostly nature or mostly whatever nurturing could be done on occasional Thursday evenings, and almost every other weekend? Whatever it was, I evolved myself from Eric Elie to L. Eric Elie to Lolis Eric Elie. My reasoning was simple. I can name a dozen Erics off the top of my head. Not so with our name.

I didn't understand what it meant to be a single mother until I dated one. I realized something then. Being in the house with a child who needs or wants something is very different from fielding the occasional phone request. Making plans for an evening or weekend or month is very different when you have someone else raising your children.

You used to boast that you only spanked me once or twice when I was a child. Had you been at home after I turned eight, who knows whether that number would have grown.

The best we can do is teach our children to not make the mistakes that we made, teach them to extend and refine whatever legacy of progress we leave them. You progressed from Scotch and water to white zinfandel to Champagne. Still, when you were asked the vintage of that gift bottle of Dom Perignon you opened that time, your response was, "Vintage? It's Dom Perignon, nigga!" I still smile when I think of that, but my taste in Champagne is more esoteric now. Perhaps your grandson's palate will be so sophisticated that he'll know the vintage of the wine without having to read the label.

You loved having flowers around, though you never had much patience for the work of gardening—the weeding and tilling and such. Maybe Niriko will learn to love caring for flowers as much as he loves the flowers themselves.

And if the family business is indeed something in the social services, maybe he will learn the arts of compromise and de-escalation, as neither you nor I managed to. Maybe he will temper his radicalism to be more practical; after all, the great American contribution to western philosophy is pragmatism.

When I moved back to New Orleans to write a column for the *Times-Picayune*, people would recognize my name and tell me they knew you from Dillard University, or the Dryades Street YMCA, or the courtroom, or the civil rights movement, or Mason's Las Vegas Strip on South Claiborne Avenue. Perhaps the people who didn't like you or respect you never bothered to speak of you to me. But those who did speak to me, without exception, spoke highly of you.

We don't know much about the history of our name. You told me that your great grandmother, Mamie Jones, named your uncle after Lolis, a teacher who came to New Roads, Louisiana, our ancestral homeland. Uncle Lolis played trumpet and died mysteriously in Chicago. You never knew him. Then there was you, Lolis Edward, who begat me, Lolis Eric, who begat Lolis Niriko.

It's a short history. Still, I hope that your grandson will come to realize that this name, our name, is an honorable name. A proud name. Who knows? Perhaps one day, like me, he'll stop calling himself by his middle name and choose to cast his lot audibly with the Lolis Elies who have come before.

# Fragments from the Long Game

KATE CARROLL DE GUTES

My mother sobs. Mucus courses out of her nose and over her upper lip, while her bottom lip turns down—as, in a trick of genetics, does mine and one of my sister's when we really weep.

My mom pulls some Kleenex out of the sleeve of her shirt and wipes at her lip, blows her nose. More Kleenex. Still more. Dabbing below her eyes and the lashes that she no longer strokes with daily mascara. She doesn't remember that she no longer applies makeup except for special events, things like doctor's visits or dinner at a brewpub, and so she carefully presses the Kleenex beneath her eyes to lift—rather than smear—the mascara she forgets is not there.

I sit across from her, in my grandmother's wingback chair that now belongs to my mother and soon will be mine. I sit in that chair—the one piece of furniture in her 550-square-foot assisted living apartment that is free from the reek of urine—and tears run down my cheeks too.

She throws her hands in the air and says, "Why am I crying?" Then she looks closely at me and says, "Why are *we* crying?"

Oh Alzheimer's, your gift to my mother is forcing her to finally live in the perpetual present tense.

"We were talking about assisted suicide and whether I had enough drugs to kill you," I say. As an afterthought, I add, "I do."

"What?" My mother has this dramatic way of shouting that word, her voice gliding up three-quarters of an octave to the "t" in *what* and then another quarter of an octave to the question mark. "I don't want to die. Why would I want to die?"

I do the only sane thing I can in the moment: I laugh and cry at the same time. "Because you have Alzheimer's, Mom."

"I do?" Her eyebrow rises in suspicion.

"Yes. And you said you didn't want to live like this."

"Well, I certainly don't want to die." And for a moment, there is my mother, sounding all Edina, Minnesota, patrician, emphasis on *certainly*, outrage on *die*.

"Okay, Mom." What else is there to say? I practice being in the moment every time we are together.

"Oh honey," she says, and starts crying again. "You've got to write this down. Maybe my story can help someone else."

The cause is no longer controversial. According to the Mayo Clinic, "Scientists believe that for most people, Alzheimer's disease is caused by a combination of genetic, lifestyle, and environmental factors that affect the brain over time. Less than 5 percent of Alzheimer's is caused by specific genetic changes that virtually guarantee a person will develop the disease."

Controversy ensues when you begin talking about a cure. Actually, there isn't a cure—which is to say there isn't a pill that prevents or arrests the disease. Only a few believe that lifestyle changes can "patch the holes in the roof," to borrow a phrase from Dr. Dale Bredsen, author of *The End of Alzheimer's*. Depending on which scientist you ask, the following may or may not help prevent Alzheimer's: balancing hormones; correcting blood ratios of zinc to copper and Omega 6 to Omega 3 acids; decreasing inflammation levels; eating a Mediterranean diet; eliminating dairy and grains; increasing exercise and searching out social interactions; improving insulin resistance; maintaining optimal weight and developing good sleep habits; taking supplements, including vitamin D, L-Carnitine, Methyl-B vitamins; treating depression; and controlling diabetes and sleep apnea.

My mother worried her entire life about Alzheimer's. It's as if she had a premonition. She tried different "cures" and changing her habits to combat the monster stalking her. But she couldn't seem to sustain them. She never sustained changes in her diet—cake with a side salad for lunch was her favorite; never kept up an exercise regimen, starting and stopping yoga, walking, the parcourse, or in the early years, Jack LaLanne on our black-and-white television. For a while she tried meditation at night after we three kids and my father had gone to bed, but more often than not, her meditation was chain-smoking Kools and watching Johnny Carson.

There is a picture I keep in a magnetic frame on my refrigerator. The photo was snapped the summer of my junior year, when I was home from university. My mom and I were about to leave for lunch at Rancho Nicasio, a Northern California roadhouse shaded by oaks that wouldn't die from the gall for another thirty years. I always loved this place because it felt like the California of my childhood—no new subdivisions scraped into the greenbelt, just the original, funky old houses with single-pane windows enclosing sagging front porches.

In the picture, I stand on my mother's right, my own right arm crossing my body to rest on her elbow, which is also bent at a right angle and crossing her body. Both of us appear uncomfortable with the size of our stomachs. My sister Sue poses half a step in front of our mom, looking back at her, grinning and hamming it up. My smile, however, looks a little grim, and I imagine that's because it's after 1:00 p.m. and I am starving. Although my mother never arrived late for work, she could not manage to leave the house for anything else before 2:00 p.m. I attribute this to a lifetime of working the p.m. nursing shift, 3:00 to 11:00. Looking at this picture and my inauthentic smile, I am certain it's late and I'm hungry.

When we were finally seated at Rancho Nicasio, I likely exhaled and listened to the white noise of the creek while studying the menu for something heavy with protein and fat, my meal of choice when I weighed ninety pounds more than I do now. I imagine my mom said what she almost always said in these situations, "Oh, let's just get a salad and a big, gooey dessert!"

Each time she said this, it sounded conspiratorial to me, like we were trying to put something over on the culture guards who insisted women keep their hunger in check—which seemed ridiculous because clearly, neither one of us was putting over anything on anyone. I mean, just look at us.

My mother was probably already insulin resistant, meaning sugar couldn't get to her cells because her insulin receptors were ignoring both the sugar and the insulin coursing through her blood. So, ironically, her cells were "starving" from lack of glucose, while the increased insulin caused the sugar to be stored immediately as fat. Of *course* she wanted dessert. I want dessert just writing about this. Give me a gluten-free lemon Bundt cake or some Swedish cream with a raspberry reduction. Serve it up to me with a latte made with whole milk—also loaded with simple carbohydrates. Truth is, I'm no different than my mother.

Two items my mother eliminated from her diet and routine in the hope of staving off Alzheimer's:

1. Farberware aluminum cookware, based on the myth, later disproven, that aluminum use led to Alzheimer's. But she only gave up aluminum for a short time, temporarily replacing it with pans coated in Teflon, which has been shown to cause a host of other issues.

2. Lipton's Instant Iced Tea, hot tea, and sun tea. This is not as foolish as it might sound because tea contains naturally occurring aluminum. However, when I google "Tea/Alzheimer's," the first link that appears is a longitudinal study of 975 tea drinkers published by the *Journal of Nutrition, Health, and Aging* and cited by the *Journal of the American Medical Association*. The study finds exactly the opposite of the 1970s theory, showing instead that tea reduced by 86 percent the risk of Alzheimer's for women with the ApoE4 gene that leads to early onset. How it helps is not known yet, but the hypothesis is that the anti-inflammatory qualities of the flavonoids in tea protect the brain and L-theanine regulates neurotransmitter activity. There is also some suggestion that tea has anti-beta-amyloid properties.

Three items she did not give up:

1. Sugar. Type 2 diabetics like my mother are naturally wired to crave sugar. My mother's blood sugar likely was elevated for years. At sixty-two, she collapsed before a dinner party while putting the finishing touches on her back-combed hair, a three times around the head shellacking of Tresemmé hairspray. Upon admission to the hospital, her blood sugar registered 440. Normal is 70 to 90.

2. Smoking. My mother smoked for fifty-two years—right until two weeks before her heart attack, which required her to spend six hours on a bypass machine as the surgeon rerouted five arteries. The aftermath: Seven weeks in the ICU, eight weeks in a skilled nursing facility, and secondary infections of MRSA, MRSE, and klebsiella pneumonia, which were treated daily for nine months with vancomycin. Oh, and a chest wound that didn't close for more than twenty-four months because healing is impeded when blood sugar climbs above 180 (see point 1).

3. Debilitating ennui. My mother, who was first an ICU nurse and then a psych nurse, told herself that "normal people" could pull themselves up by their bootstraps and did not need antidepressants. By "normal people," she meant herself. The meds were fine for anybody else. Her depression, however, she deemed "situational," as if it would resolve unaided. But years and years of situational depression left her chronically depressed. She always sounded surprised when I reminded her that just two weeks of situational depression causes bootstrap-resistant chemical changes in the brain.

I don't know when my mother began to manifest symptoms of Alzheimer's. I do remember being a teenager and watching her in our kitchen, the receiver of the avocado-green wall phone cradled between her left ear and shoulder, its spiral cord stretched across the kitchen to the table where she sits talking to her mother. To my mother's left on the table a footed, gray ceramic coffee mug rests on a leather coaster she brought back from Mexico City. To her right is a blue-gray ashtray with a Kool cigarette burning in it. The phone cord—easily fifteen feet long—runs under her arm so that when we pass through the kitchen we can lift it and walk under on our way to the family room, the backyard, or the garage. I can see my mom at the table. I can see her in blue Bermuda shorts—really nylon pants cut off at the knee, my mother skateboarder/cyclist-hip thirty years early—and one of my father's discarded, oversized oxford cloth shirts, likely with a brown-edged hole on the sleeve where an errant ash from his Pall Mall had dropped during some business dinner.

My mom constantly reminded me that she called her mother every morning at 8:30 Pacific, after ushering my two sisters and me off to school. She told me that she worried to her mother again and again about her memory. And Sue remembers our mother telling her that our grandmother reassured our mother that of course she forgot things: she was busy juggling three kids and an alcoholic husband. My grandmother told my mother she'd remember the important things, which I took to mean names, dates of birth, big accomplishments.

I don't know what my mother forgot back then. Plots of novels? Actors in movies? Names of people she just met? Appointments? Say I was fourteen when this started happening: my mother would have been forty-two, right about the time that perimenopause hits, one symptom of which is forgetfulness and concentration issues. But maybe she forgot more than the usual? Maybe instead of just losing the keys to the car, she sometimes forgot how to use the keys? Maybe she found items in random spots? It's hard to know because my father routinely lost items such as his keys, his pocketknife, his glasses, his wallet. When he'd locate them in weird places, he'd say to one of us, "That's your mother's doing." How many of her memory worries were actually gaslighting by him?

A few things I routinely forget:

1. Details and titles of books. I never forget the author's name or what the cover looks like, however.
2. The year my mother died. This last one I attribute to launching my

first book only two months before she died, immediately writing and launching a second book, and an ongoing confusion as to seasons and years. Is it April or August? January or June? 2017 or 2018? So, I excuse myself that I sometimes cannot remember if she died in August 2015 or August 2016.

3. Appointments. Even with a "tiny computer" in my pocket—what my mother called my phone—I forget conference calls with clients or coffee with friends, or I fail to enter a meeting, or I say yes to something before checking the calendar and double-book.

4. People. Their names or that we've even met. I find this last bit the most disconcerting. My hair is a distinctive gray, and I wear bow ties to all arts events. A smiling genderqueer woman in a tie is memorable, and the number of people coming up to me at events—my own or others'—is substantial. They expect I'll remember them either because we've met before or they've friended me on Facebook. I've started categorizing the Facebook people into "Real Writers," by which I mean literary darlings or people with books; "New Writers," who are writers I've met who don't have books or people who have taken a class from me; and "Fans," the people who read my work and reach out. Before events I study the lists, look closely at the faces and names of those I'm fairly certain I've met multiple times. It's my version of *The Devil Wears Prada* assistant whispering in my ear as each person approaches.

Here is a scene: I'd spent the afternoon writing, in that liminal space between worlds where you are listening to the muse with one ear cocked toward the heavens and yet staying tethered slightly to this corporeal plane by keeping one leg wrapped around the chair. Except maybe I hadn't held on as tightly as I should. Because when I walked over to the neighbor's porch sit—a summertime ritual they host once a month—I still felt, I don't know, quite in my head, which is sometimes a way of saying not quite in my body. I pushed opened the picket fence gate that hangs askew so that it dragged loudly across the front walk, and all heads turned toward me—including Sylvia's. She sat in a straight-backed chair, old school with perfect posture and a beatific smile—the edges of her blue eyes crinkling—a butterfly bush hanging over her, its purple flowers dancing in and out of her mess of auburn curls.

"Hey, Martha," I said. I knew that wasn't quite right, but the truth was, every time I'd looked at Sylvia for the past month, at the gym, at a handful of readings we'd been to, I'd had to repeat her name in my head: *Sylvia, Sylvia, Sylvia.* To remind myself that her name was Sylvia and not Martha, the name of her partner. I'd never gotten them confused before. I chalked the confusion up to seeing them separately where normally they were a unit, doing everything together.

Yet it came out of my mouth. "Hey, Martha." It took a beat, a flash of surprise or consternation or confusion crossing Sylvia's face before I said, "I mean Sylvia." Then I laughed. "Sylvia, Martha, Martha, Sylvia. You two are a single entity in my mind, apparently."

I went home and called my sort-of girlfriend, sobbed as I told her the story. She listened, and unlike previous friends or lovers, I didn't feel like she was rolling her eyes. I could feel her kindness through the ethers, and her pragmatism too. She was also already multitasking on Google.

"Alright, listen," she said, all business, adamant about not being interrupted. "Do you have trouble knowing the date, month, or year?"

"Sometimes," I said. "You know time has always been sort of a mystery to me."

"Okay, that's no," she laughed and continued. "Do you become disoriented in unfamiliar places?"

"Only when I'm on book tour and I can't remember where the bathroom is in whatever hotel or Airbnb I'm in."

"Okay, that's a no too. Do you have trouble handling money like tips or change?"

An easy no.

The questions went on with me answering no or giving plausible reasons why, for instance, I might not remember to pay my bills on time: "I'm in the middle of a remodel, and I'm working at the dining room table instead of my desk."

"Remember our agreement?" she asked me.

"Which one?" I was about to say, *see I do have memory loss*, but she jumped on the end of the sentence before I could even get it out.

"The one where you die of a heart attack at home, in your bed, at ninety, after a long bike ride? That's our agreement. Just keep repeating that. You're fine. Really. I promise."

Let me tell you how often between the ages of forty-eight and fifty-two—before I sucked up my fear and allowed my doctor to draw a vial of blood to see if I carried the ApoE4 gene—I worried that my memory issues were not perimenopausal but early onset Alzheimer's, which typically starts in your forties or fifties.

Turns out I don't have that gene. But according to the rest of the blood tests recommended by Alzheimer's expert Bredsen, I do have other markers that could lead to Alzheimer's: increased homocysteine levels, the wrong ratio of Omega 6 to Omega 3 acids, too much copper to zinc, low glutathione levels. My doctor, a believer in the thirty-six-point Bredsen plan to arrest or prevent Alzheimer's, urges me to adopt not all thirty-six points, but many of them—just for three months and then we'll retest. So, right before the holidays I eliminated alcohol, dairy, and grains. I was already strength training two times a week and cardio two other times, and now I've added two more workouts and a handful of additional meds and supplements.

Just as my mother's Alzheimer's forced me to stay present with her, make no plans, this plan also insists I live in the moment. I can't think about doing this the rest of my life. Because the reality is, you can do everything right, at least for a while, but playing the long game when you're forty-three or fifty-three—as I am now—is difficult to sustain. The challenge is connecting cream in my coffee today or three cookies tomorrow to a demise horizon-point twenty or thirty years from now: the incontinence, the terror and confusion of where you are located in time and space, the sundowner's syndrome, the loss of words and sometimes meaning itself. I wonder, How can this glass of wine and this eggplant

moussaka really ruin my life? But they can and they may. And my sisters
and I don't have children, so who will care for me, for them? Will we wind
up in a state-run nursing home with no one to advocate for us? Maybe.

Here is another scene: A woman I am in love with has told me she is not
in love with me because she's uncertain—if she's gay, if our attraction
means something, if, if, if. It's a complex story involving two coasts,
lots of long intimate letters full of Eros, and a whirlwind six-week affair
in Portland. I am shouting at her inside my head and not remotely in
the present moment. I am also dressed to the nines, having just come
from a design agency's Christmas party where three straight women
flirted shamelessly with my bow-tied, bespectacled self. Now, I must
go to Safeway and shop for a brunch I'm hosting the next morning. The
last brunch I hosted was with her, the two of us at opposite ends of my
great-grandparents' oak table, catching each other's eye, smiling, mixing
our friends together. So, I'm heartbroken, it's late, and I feel toyed with
by women on both coasts.

The front of my black shopping cart causes the doors of the store to
whoosh open and, as I step inside, continuing my "conversation" with
the woman not in love with me and not even on this coast, I manage to
catch a real live woman smiling at me, all white teeth and dimples. She
sing-songs, "Hi, Kate!"

I am hurled into the present moment where I have no idea who this
woman is. None.

"Hey," I reply. "How's it going?" I don't wait for an answer. I push on
my cart and say aloud, "You do not have Alzheimer's. You're wearing a
bow tie. *You have a bow tie, not Alzheimer's.*"

I pick up eggs, veggies, half-and-half for the coffee drinkers, and
a bottle of red wine. I go home; I open the wine and pour myself a
huge glass. I should probably mention that at the Christmas party I
also drank expensive red wine and ate eggplant moussaka loaded with
melted gouda cheese.

The long game. My mother. Alzheimer's. I am no better. I always felt disappointed and—can I say this about a dead parent?—a little angry when I witnessed her failed attempts at self-preservation. I felt so diligent, so different. Looking at that self slumped on the couch and holding a pint-sized Mason jar of red wine, all I feel now is compassion and chagrin.

Here is the final scene of this essay: it could be any place where my mother is with my sisters or me, years before she ever receives a diagnosis of Alzheimer's. Imagine one of us telling her a story from our life. The story doesn't matter except that it is something we want her to hear, to acknowledge. We all long for her to *recognize* us. But instead of truly responding to what we are telling her, she will say, "Did I ever tell you about the time that I . . ." And it will be a story we've heard before, it will be a story in which she stars, it will be a story that is only glancingly relevant to what my sisters or I were just talking about, it will be a story about something that occurred before any of us were born.

Usually, it relates to the days she worked in San Francisco as an ICU nurse at Kaiser on Geary Street. We know the patients, their diagnoses, their names—this, almost half a century before HIPPA—we know the names of the janitors and aides too. We know where she lived—in the apartment on Jackson or the walk-up on Washington (with the neighborhood mynah bird that whistled at her)—we know with whom she lived. Else it will be a story about Drexel, the house her mother, her brother, and she moved to after her father died.

What I'm saying is, it will be about the past.

I don't know if my mom realized how much of her life she lived in the past. I don't know that I recognized it until I saw how much I lived in the future: *when I lose weight, when I'm physically stronger, when that woman finally realizes she wants me, when my third book goes viral.* It took my heart being broken repeatedly to force me into the present.

Mostly. Because as a writer, I spend so much time mulling, looking for meaning, that often I fail to fathom how far away from the here and now I've wandered. Like the moment in Safeway, I must continually pull myself back to the present. This has become one of my mother's greatest gifts to me, this remembering to be in the ever-present now—not the past, not the future—breaking the family pattern, and not viewing the constant redirection back to the present moment as a failure, but as course correction toward some point on my horizon that I can't see and, if I am living in the present moment, am not yet supposed to see.

# Self-Made Men

LELAND CHEUK

Fifteen years ago, when I was twenty-seven, I sat with my mom and dad in the conference room of a law firm overlooking Union Square in San Francisco and tried to get them divorced.

Months before, my mom had called me on the phone, sobbing. She told me she had followed my dad in her car and discovered him on a date with a woman my age. I wasn't exactly sure why this latest assignation—there had been others—triggered such an emotional response. When I was a kid, they'd often fought (sometimes physically) over my father's serial philandering. I was nine or ten when I accompanied him on an outing with a woman who was not my mother. They took me to Chuck E. Cheese, where, over pizza and Skee-Ball, I wondered why we were hanging out together, behaving as a family would. After fun times for this kid, the adults then had fun times in this woman's home while I roamed the garage, alone. I had always assumed that despite my father's behavior, staying in the marriage was my mother's choice.

In that conference room, while the middle-aged attorney explained the concepts of community property and alimony, my mom couldn't stop crying, and my dad managed only the occasional mumbled response, refusing to meet my gaze. The rage I had felt while listening to my mom's weeks of disconsolate phone calls dissipated when I saw my dad in person. I actually felt guilty for forcing his indiscretions into the light. I didn't know anything about his views on love and matrimony. Perhaps he never loved my mother. Perhaps this other woman was his One True Love. For all I knew, I was only complicating his path to a long-delayed state of true domestic happiness. I had hired a divorce attorney because I feared, as my retired mother did, that my father was not above leaving her penniless.

Everyone in the room assumed I was 100 percent on my mother's side, but I'm ashamed to admit that I couldn't help but cast sympathetic glances at the rumpled and ill-at-ease villain in our family drama. He didn't look like the towering, swaggering demon that my mother described. He was just my dad, embarrassed and ashamed. Perhaps because, among other reasons, he could no longer claim to be a role model for his oldest son.

My father is the American immigrant ideal of the mythic self-made man.

By the time he was my age now (forty-two), he had two kids and a multimillion-dollar net worth from owning and landlording several homes in Northern California. While working as a hardware engineer at a large telecom company in Silicon Valley, he studied on weekends to get his real estate broker's license and started his own company. By the time I was a teen, my parents, my younger brother, and I lived in a three-thousand-square-foot house in the affluent suburb of Cupertino, the home of Apple Inc. Almost annually, my dad bought a new Mercedes, because they were "safer." He'd *made it*, as the saying goes. Today, at seventy, he's one of the few tech workers his age still working. When I ask why he hasn't retired, he says, "The job is pretty easy."

His life certainly wasn't always so easy. In 1976, when my father was twenty-seven, he arrived in America from China by way of Hong Kong. He was five foot seven and just ninety-nine pounds, according to his first passport. Black-and-white photos of him as a young man show him nearly starved, his eyes sunken, and his cheekbones and Adam's apple his most prominent features from the neck up. He didn't even have a high school education. In 1957 his father had been labeled a rightist for being associated with anticommunist literary groups and was sent to a rural reeducation camp, where he did hard labor such as toting water into coal mines. The family was split up, and my uncle and my twenty-one-year-old father were also exiled to remote areas in South China: my uncle to a swamp infested with "snail fever," a parasitic disease, and my father to an army reclamation farm on Hainan Island.

My mother describes her early courtship with my father as being "in a fog." She characterizes him as the big talker with grand ambitions, while she was the "know-nothing little girl" who enjoyed drawing and playing music—the youngest of eleven (her father had two wives) in a well-off family. Soon after my parents had met in their early twenties, in the middle of the Cultural Revolution, my dad made it clear he had no intention of starving in China. Together, they trained for their escape, which involved a perilous crossing of the Pearl River estuary to Hong Kong, by wading in local rivers with makeshift floating devices strapped to their waists. The swim took all night, in waters that were shark-infested, with visibility so poor that one could be easily swept out to sea. To get to the estuary, they hiked for two weeks, day and night, through hills and wilderness, avoiding snakes and wild dogs, as well as border patrols and their canines.

My father almost didn't survive the swim. He fell unconscious from hypothermia and my mom dragged him ashore, their legs and feet sliced up from the rocks. She was afraid that the mainland Chinese border guards were after them, but she wasn't strong enough to carry my dad to the safety of the customs station. A friendly fisherman offered his boat as refuge and nursed my father back to consciousness with ginger tea. Once recuperated, they crossed the border into Hong Kong, then a British colony, and applied for asylum. Some of my parents' cohorts weren't so lucky. Hundreds of thousands of young Chinese tried this swim between 1956 and 1980; they became known as "freedom swimmers." Countless young people drowned or were shot and killed or detained, beaten, and sent back to work camps.

According to my mother, she saved my father's life.

He claims that if she had been a faster swimmer, he wouldn't have been in the water so long and, thus, wouldn't have fallen ill.

According to my grandfather, my dad had a natural affinity for electronics. When he was just a child, he fixed my grandmother's broken transistor radio. Once in Hong Kong, he got an entry-level electrical engineering job. After he immigrated to America, armed with only a recommendation from his Hong Kong employer, he was hired at a large computer manufacturer.

My father often said that to survive and thrive, you had to be *goo-wak*, which in Cantonese means at best "clever" and at worst "devious." Occasionally, when I would get a B in school or be unwilling to work in his real estate office on weekends, he would threaten to send me back to China, where I'd have to use my wits to survive. The implications of this threat were that (1) Americans were soft and easy marks—the country's "freedom" made life easier to game—and (2) my father had overcome his youth of persecution and poverty by his wits alone.

As one might guess about someone who risked his life to start a new one in a foreign country, risk has never bothered my father. He never blinked an eye at getting second mortgages and spinning those funds into more investment properties. When I worked for him, assembling mortgage applications for his customers, if we were missing a letter of approval, he'd just ask me to type one up. Then he'd forge the applicant's signature, barely even trying to emulate the person's handwriting, betting that the bank's underwriters wouldn't notice. He's made investments that didn't work out and left him cash-strapped for years at a time. He's been sued on numerous occasions by unhappy business partners. And of course, cheating on one's wife repeatedly requires a certain level of risk tolerance.

My father embodies all dimensions of the American dream—positive and negative. The self-made man can come to America with nothing and become financially successful, earning a life of privilege for himself and his family. But he cannot just be good at his job; he must have two or more jobs. The self-made man cannot just follow the rules; he must be devious. He must always be focused on the next new thing: the next new country, the next new business opportunity, the next new house, the next new car, the next new wife, the next new family. He cannot focus too long on the people who may have helped him along the way. The self-made man can only be so loyal, because above all, his desires can be neither denied nor sated.

Did my dad become this person because of or in spite of becoming American? Has he misinterpreted or simply distilled and absorbed American values?

I'm not sure I'll ever know.

The divorce attorney discerned during the discovery process that my father had shuttered his real estate business and started it anew by opening accounts under his name and leaving out my mother's so that he could argue that she wasn't entitled to his "new" business, which was established *after* the date of their separation. My mother raged in emails to my father, cc-ing me, that she couldn't believe she had married such a "snake person."

I can't remember a time when my father and I were close. Maybe that's why I couldn't resist at least glimpsing his side in my parents' divorce battle. Deep down, I wished to be close to him. I wanted to forgive his sins. Isn't that what love is? A predisposition to airbrushing someone's worst flaws?

I like to think that my father tried to be a good dad. His attempts come to me in flashes. Him teaching me to ride a bike on our traffic-less suburban street. Him playing basketball with me at my grade school playground. Him beating me at Ping-Pong in the rec room of his employer's office building. My brother and I never had to work through college like other students; my dad took care of our tuition and living expenses. When I wanted to move into San Francisco after I had graduated from Berkeley, he emptied his rental property in the city, renovated it, and let me live there rent-free for over a decade. Then, of course, there were all those "safer" luxury cars my dad handed down to us.

I like to think that I tried to be the son he wanted. When I was in seventh grade, I collected and sold baseball cards. Once I hid a creased corner on a valuable rookie card with my thumb and sold it to an unsuspecting mark for way more than it was worth only to have him chase me around our junior high demanding a refund when he discovered the card wasn't in mint condition. I was trying to be like my father. I was trying to be *goo-wak*. In college, I resisted my creative impulses and unenthusiastically majored in business, a move in which my father delighted.

My dad has always voted Republican. Lower taxes, he explained. (Yes, my mom and I believe he voted for Trump.) In his home office, he even kept a golden mallet gifted by Ronald Reagan's campaign thanking him for a donation. In my junior-high graphic arts class, I traced images of George H. W. Bush on magazine covers and made fun of kids by calling them Democrats.

By high school, it dawned on me that something was off about my family. My dad was rarely home. My parents slept in separate bedrooms. I avoided inviting friends over because I felt tense in the family house. When I tried to rationalize how our family had become so unhappy, naturally I traced it back to the way my father treated my mother.

When I was just four, my dad was working on schematics on the dining room table, and my mom served me a bowl of Jell-O with milk. Somehow the milk spilled, wetting my dad's papers, and he grew so angry that he tried to execute a flying kick upon my mom like Ryu in *Street Fighter*. He missed, but whipping out Jackie Chan moves upon defenseless women was not beyond my dad's particular version of the pale.

When, behind closed doors, my mom made too much of a fuss about my dad's chronic infidelity, he would hit her. My mom would scream, sometimes just for help, but sometimes for someone to "save her life." The next day I'd see the bruises on her arms. My brother and I would hear the altercations in our shared room across the hall. During one of the many fights, when I was eight and he was six, he crawled into my bed and said in Cantonese, "I'm scared."

"Me too," I replied.

That's the only time I remember us speaking Cantonese to each other.

In my parents' harsher, more openly patriarchal generation, domestic violence, philandering, and verbal abuse were accepted. No one on my dad's side of the family called him out on his behavior, but they did nickname my mother Fat Eight, because she was the eighth sister in her family and, during that time, she was a little plump. We had every material comfort my parents could have dreamed of when they embarked across the Pearl River estuary, but simple decency eluded us.

Over thirty years later, I still have nightmares about my parents' fights. And I feel guilt that I never did anything to help my mom. The closest I've come to standing up to my father was when I tried to get them divorced.

Fourteen years later, my parents are still married.

In the end, my mom didn't want to be protected from my father. As the process of uncovering the family's finances dragged on, thanks to Dad's delaying tactics, Mom stopped responding to the attorney's emails, complaining that the fees were too expensive. When I reasoned that the work was necessary and that once the alimony payments were agreed upon, she could be free of my dad both financially and emotionally, my mom just started weeping quietly. She didn't want to be free. She wanted to be taken care of. She wanted to be protected *by* my father, not from him, the man she had pulled out of the Pearl River decades before.

In exchange for being financially cared for on a day-to-day basis by my father, my mother paid a stiff price. Because their finances were still intermingled, Dad withdrew $180,000 of the inheritance Mom received from her mother's death and used it as a down payment on the house where he and his girlfriend live today—an ungentlemanly move about which my mother frequently rages. She now lives in that three-thousand-square-foot house in Cupertino, alone.

I've never met my father's girlfriend. I have no idea whether they plan to marry one day or have children. From my mom, I hear that he travels the world with his girlfriend during the holidays, which is why his presence at family events tends to be scarce around Thanksgiving and Christmas. I don't even know for sure whether they haven't had children. I may very well one day meet my stepsiblings.

My father has always been my lodestar—sort of. I've looked at what he's done in his life and tried to do the opposite. I'm happily and faithfully married and childless. I never wanted to become a parent, because *good*

*God, look what happened to mine*. I walked away from a lucrative business career in exchange for the far lower financial ceiling of being a writer. When my novel first came out in the United States, I stated in several interviews that the villainous, abusive father / small-town demagogue in the book was loosely based on my father. I've long considered myself, if not the better version of him, then at least more *evolved*.

And yet, in recent years, my dad has made it harder to simply run from his moral universe.

As my father's parents aged into their nineties, he took primary responsibility for their care, while his older brother kept his distance from the end-of-life ugliness. My grandparents lived just a twenty-minute drive away from my dad after he sponsored their immigration to the United States in 1980. He has been the one to usher his parents to emergency rooms in the middle of the night. He's been the one to coordinate the caretaker schedules for my Alzheimer's-stricken grandmother. He was the one feeding and cleaning up after my cancer-stricken grandfather in the weeks before his death. He planned every aspect of my grandfather's funeral, from the eulogies to the cremation and disposal of his ashes.

"Tell me what you think of this," Dad said to me before the funeral. "I was thinking of using an airplane to drop his ashes over a vineyard." His voice cracked as he added, "He couldn't breathe for two or three minutes before he died. In the fresh air, he'll be able to breathe."

I told him I thought it was a great idea.

"I'd like the same to be done for me," he said. "When I'm not here."

I knew he was telling me this because I'm the oldest son. Just as my younger brother had been spared all of my mother's tear-sodden phone calls about my dad's sex life, I was receiving the first of my assignments related to his late life. It was one of the first times he talked to me about something other than the next real estate investment, the next job, the next material score. The afterlife was now the next, new thing.

When I spoke to my grandfather in his final months, he told me that my dad had been the ideal son. I doubt very much that my father feels the same way about me. Will I so willingly play the role of the dutiful son, after all that I've witnessed? Will I be there when he needs me most? I can't truthfully say yes with certainty. And yet, if I am indeed the better person, shouldn't I be able to?

My grandfather's last wishes were to (1) see my first novel translated and published in China and (2) return to Guangzhou one last time with his entire family to celebrate the launch of my book and show his grand-children and great-grandchildren their ancestral roots. Two months before his death, he still held out hope, even as his cancer advanced.

"My leg isn't feeling great," he told me over the phone. "I'm not sure I'll be able to walk if we go." As the weeks passed and the steep decline began, I realized he had just been talking about his leg so he wouldn't have to talk about the inevitable.

The book is now off to the printers, and my dad is making the family China trip happen, coordinating schedules and paying for large chunks of it. Even though my grandfather won't be there, my dad is willing his last wishes into existence, like countless other achievements in my father's life. He knows my book is about a very dysfunctional family. He knows he inspired the book's antagonist. And yet, he's never shown anything but happiness that the book exists.

I don't know what to make of my father's latest magnanimities. Is he trying to make up for the past? More likely this is part of who he's always been, and I've spent half a lifetime focusing on his most lurid deeds. I've run from him, made him the ultimate villain in my life, and even tried to divorce him, but now it seems inevitable that we'll become closer in coming years. That's the thing about lodestars—they're always in your sky.

# The Nut Doesn't Fall Far from the Fucking Nut Tree

**S. BEAR BERGMAN**

When I turned fourteen years old away at boarding school, I paid for my meal with a credit card for the first time. I'd been authorized to use this new parent-issued credit card, given to me for purchasing train tickets and preapproved supplies, to have a nice lunch on my birthday with a few of my brand-new school friends. We ate at a place people seemed to like, charmingly in an old firehouse, and when the bill came, I paid it—wrote in the tip, totaled the bill, signed, kept my copy, and so on. My new friends sort of blinked at me. Later, at the dorm, one asked how long I'd had my own credit card.

"A week?" I answered. "It just came."

"Oh," she said. Later in the year she confessed that she'd asked because I had handled it all quite smoothly and she was very impressed by me in the moment. The truth was I hadn't been concerned about what to do. For good or ill—and sometimes for both—I just did it how my father did. Since I was, at the time, understood by the world to be a fourteen-year-old girl, having mannerisms and habits that were suitable to a forty-five-year-old businessman caused consternation at frequent intervals. I addressed clerks and shopkeepers with his bumptious charm; I put on my coat and crossed my legs and settled myself in chairs with his movements, the wide-angled grace of the big guy I eventually became; I shook my head reprovingly when I didn't like what the speaker was saying. I still do all of these things, but having transitioned into a man, it seems less off-puttingly incongruous now. One trait seemed somehow to fit all and none of the categories, though: my father's skill, which I also grew into, as a storyteller.

Every night at dinner, my father would tell stories from his day. They were mostly small, quotidian workday stories, but sometimes if he was in a good-enough mood, my brother and I could coax him into telling family stories or favorites from his work life or from college. What we noticed was that it improved his mood too. To fall into the cadences of story, even grumpily at first, is also an experience I have now, and it remains an incredibly satisfying one. And at every gathering, whether a holiday dinner or Shabbat collation, at a cookout or a birthday party, on line at the store, waiting for a train, while taking a tour of my future high school when the tour guide was talking and we were supposed to be listening—Dad, come *on*—there were always stories.

My dad, who's a numbers guy, can't write at all. My uncle—my father's brother and only sibling—can: He's a well-regarded gay writer and poet with a long and distinguished publication record. We move in some of the same circles now, and depending on their generation, people might ask me if I might be related to him or occasionally whether he's related to me. But my father can't write at all; his attempts to prepare a speech for some occasion are inevitably an unrelieved block of short, simple, declarative sentences that read like an intermediate English language learner writing a final assignment for a communications class. But that's on paper.

In person, it's a different ballgame. In exactly the way that children of English professors effortlessly learn perfect grammar and never to misuse lie for lay, I learned perfect comedic timing and the lapidary art of composing a story. To compose a story is quite like composing a photograph—there's art and craft in what one chooses as the center of the image, what's kept in and what's cropped out, the angle, the light. I learned from a million hours of observation of the kind that only a child can lavish on a parent how to string together a scatter of details to make a coherent narrative, how to pace the action from beat to beat, how to read the room to make sure people were following and not move too quickly but neither too slow; how to show the heart of a story—the actual message, the flaw that reveals the perfection—at just the right moment.

I learned the facial and bodily grammar that adds a layer of depth and nuance to the story as well, modifiers and limiters and intensifiers and even the complex linguistics of contradicting my words with my face to show the listener that I am, briefly, reporting rather than telling. That's why my father's attempts at writing seem so rudimentary—because the page only tells a portion of the story. Without the tone, inflection, pacing and other communicative information that come when he tells a story to a group, the words themselves seem like struggling seedlings outside a new house, bare and stunted. For my part, I solve the same problem in the exact opposite way: I use punctuation in all type and manner of off-label ways in order to introduce some of those elements back onto the page, as you can clearly see (unless our stalwart copy editor of this volume has cleared them away and returned me to Standard Correct American Punctuation, the floor around her desk positively littered with commas and em dashes she's banished with prejudice).

I pace my sentences on the page as they are in my head and experience no greater compliment than to be told an essay or chapter sounds just like how I talk. Natively, I am a talker, just like my father is. I love storytelling for the opportunity to be in the room with just the people I'm with, to watch how they're hearing me and give them exactly the right mix of nuance and boldness, just the perfect cocktail of illuminating explanations and flip, you-know-the-rest-of-that hand gesture. Like a high-performance engine that gets tinkered with before each race for the optimal mix of oxygen and gasoline for the track and weather, the storyteller makes thousands of tiny instinctual judgment calls in every rendition. On the page, I can only choose once, and then every reader has an off-the-rack experience. But live, in front of an audience—no matter how small—that's where I am most completely happy in my work.

My experiences of trying to study storytelling, formally, were similar to my experience of trying to study English grammar. My parents, though not professors, are well spoken in Standard American English, so I found it paradoxically difficult to reveal the process behind my mastery. I'd learned it all of a single piece, and not in stages. I could spot the error and correct an ungrammatical sentence easily during my sixth-grade language arts classes, but I struggled for years to understand tenses and cases and which the hell was the adverb (I finally got that part down, but I still don't understand gerunds, not really, not even with Dorothy Parker's help).

In the same style, I took workshops and classes in storytelling as I deepened my theater practice (my father found the idea hilarious, as though I'd confessed to taking an eight-week instructional program in Duck Duck Goose) but found them frustrating beyond words. I could never articulate well *why* I had made a particular choice or what my *rationale* was for encouraging a classmate to skip a bit or move something to the end, it just felt Correct to me that way. Certain constructions or compositions had an ineffable rightness about them that others didn't. Some sentences felt finished, satisfied, and satisfactory, and others either unfairly truncated or extended beyond their capacities, like single parents trying to manage an unreasonable number of tasks. In my head, or maybe in my blood, there exists a metronome for how a sentence should unfurl itself, and it's so deeply ingrained I've never been able to go against it, not even to save an essay or a story from being cut out of a book or a show.

Some of that is repetition. As a parent I have learned that children sometimes have to be specifically taught a thing, like riding a bicycle or addressing an envelope, a process during which you correct them and guide them and encourage them and eventually celebrate the success as a shared project. In other cases, they have to be reminded approximately eleventy million times—like saying "please" and "thank you"—before they eventually internalize it (they do eventually, right?). Those are rituals of parenting, and we do them over and over with full recognition that they're a part of the job even though it can be exhausting. They're a part of the job that many of us knew to expect, having seen other parents engage in them. But there's another entire class of learning in which children just watch and listen to you every day, day upon day, and then one day reproduce exactly what you do. Sometimes this is very exciting, like when they spontaneously pick up a spoon and eat or spontaneously critique a billboard for being sexist and ridiculous, and sometimes it might cause a person to swiftly reevaluate the kind of language they use in traffic, but my father and his friends told stories so often and with such craft, with so unimpeachable a sense that this was a foundational skill of life that I simply picked it up and ate.

(Once, an interviewer with whom I was annoyed and frustrated because of the way she constructed her questions about my gender asked me where I'd studied storytelling. I told her I'd studied with Arnold Friedlander, one of my dad's close friends and owner of a building supplies business, a gifted natural storyteller who would have hooted helplessly with mirth if anyone had suggested that storytelling was a thing a person could go to school for. The interviewer made affirmative, approving noises as if I had identified myself as having attended the Harvard of storytelling and printed this tidbit of my pedigree in her magazine.)

There are more ways that I am like my father; they are so many and myriad and idiosyncratic that when he expresses (about me) the sentiment that gives this volume its title, he does not refer to the wholesome apple but says instead *the nut doesn't fall far from the fucking nut tree*, and I assure you he means this fondly. I have his wide and friendly cheekbones and large head, his generous mouth, his mesomorphic broad-shouldered body and his wide, flat feet. I have his sense of humor and his sense of duty, more of both than a lot of people, his easy gregariousness and his work ethic and his mile-wide judgmental streak. We are both *a lot*, in every regard. There are things we don't share, too, from his disdain for beaches to his suspicion of live theater, but if I could include a video with this essay, here's what you could see if I showed both of us side by side at the beginning: both of us opening our hands up and outward, both cocking our heads slightly to the side, both pursing our lips slightly with the lower lip pooched out fractionally more, both nodding in a sort of acquiescence with a brief close of our eyes at the nadir of the nod, both looking at you, both breathing in, both beginning the story.

# The Feeding Gene

KAREN GRIGSBY BATES

It was sometime in the early sixties. Mother was an elementary school teacher, and the next day was her end-of-year class trip. I went to a different school from hers, and to the best of my knowledge, if you didn't bring or buy lunch, you didn't get lunch.

"For our class trip we had to bring our *own* lunch," I told her, as I put together yet another sandwich and added it to the stack.

"Well," Mother said, still spreading jelly, never breaking pace, "some of these children might not *have* lunch. I don't want them to go hungry while others eat, or be embarrassed that they don't have lunch. I told everybody I was bringing lunch, so everybody will have the *same* lunch."

"What if somebody doesn't like peanut butter and jelly?" my little sister, Patty, asked, wielding her own knife.

My mother stopped spreading, turned, and gave us The Look. "Then they don't have to eat it. They can wait till they get home. Anyway, it's possible someone might like two sandwiches . . ."

Mother knew her people. That afternoon she returned slightly sunburned with an empty bag.

We should not have been surprised. Our mother came from a long line of people who had inherited what we've named the Feeding Gene. She couldn't sit by and see people, especially children, hungry if she could help it.

She inherited the urge legitimately. I don't remember much about my great-grandmother Alice, but my grandmother certainly had a near-pathological need to feed people. And that, obviously, had been passed on to Mother.

After graduating with a degree in biology from Hampton University, Mother moved north, from North Carolina to New Haven, where she was trained in X-ray technology and employed by Yale's hospital. She met Daddy there and, in true 1950s fashion, stayed in her new husband's town after their wedding. The new husband may have traveled South to marry his bride, but he wasn't too particular about spending time down there, so when we visited my grandparents, usually in the summer for a few weeks, it was Mother, Patty, and me. When I was young, we'd often take the train. Going south, the Southern Crescent came into Charlotte at a civilized hour, but on the return North, it always arrived in what felt to me to be the middle of the night. Didn't matter what time it departed—my grandmother Purry would always get up a few hours before we left, fry chicken and bake biscuits so we'd have something good to eat on the long trip back home. (And perhaps because she wasn't positive we'd be allowed into the dining car, although from what I remember, we were.)

It was kind of magical to be clicking along, swaying gently with the train's bump, and at one point open a shoebox carefully lined with wax paper. Inside: Purry's exquisite fried chicken pieces, flaky biscuits, and slices of pound cake that my mother and sister seem to have mastered effortlessly as adults. (I keep trying, but I am not there yet.)

On one of those return trips, the porter lifted Patty (who was maybe three or four) from the train's platform and someone handed her the shoebox, as Mother followed behind. The box was a fancy contraption from Charlotte's fanciest shoe store. (My mother and grandmother and, alas, I all have narrow feet and regular stores often only carried medium and wide widths, so expensive shoes were a necessity, not an extravagance.) The box could open at either end via a couple of silk ropes. Somehow Patty took the box by the wrong rope, and the perfidious bottom fell open. There was a cascade of Purry's fragrant, lovingly packed offerings—Chicken! Biscuits! Cake!—spilling out onto the platform. Fortunately, everything was individually wrapped in waxed paper, so after a shocked silence, we did the sensible thing and dumped it all back into the elegant, traitorous box, after which an adult carried it to our roomette.

I thought the Feeding Gene just came from my mother's side but realized, as I got older, that Daddy had it too. If my friends were over to play in the backyard, he'd poke his head out the door and ask, "You kids want something to eat?" Of course they did. It was probably baloney sandwiches or hot dogs, maybe even crackers and cheese. But we ate it. Daddy worked close enough to home that when we were in elementary school, he came home and gave us lunch, and he told us if we had classmates who needed lunch, bring them too. When adults visited, especially single adults who might drop by after work or on a late Saturday afternoon, they were usually invited to stay for dinner. If they protested, Daddy would say, "C'mon— we'll put another plate on the table." (Easy for him to say—Mother did most of the kitchen work. But some of them were her teacher friends, and she didn't seem to mind.)

Daddy did not cook a lot except for steak and bacon; he didn't trust us not to overcook either. ("You people have two settings on the stove," he'd snort. "High and off . . ."). And also spaghetti, which was usually an all-day affair, usually on the weekend. First, he'd pull out some Italian sausages, pork and veal, studded with caraway seeds and flecks of red pepper. He'd sauté those, releasing their fat. Then the sausages were lifted out, and he'd shovel in several handfuls of onions and green peppers. (He let us help with that.) The vegetables would get stirred around in the fat until they were soft, then he'd add a couple cans of puréed tomatoes and a few tablespoons of tomato paste, a pinch of salt, and a little bit of sugar. Then the sausages would go back in, and to the best of my recollection, I swear the whole thing would simmer on a back burner for *hours*. We kids would get hungrier and hungrier, and finally it was ready. The deep-red sauce would be ladled over regular spaghetti, and we'd pass around a can of shelf-stable, grated Parmesan. (He was picky about our meat and deli, but apparently grated cheese was not on the same tier of concern. This was before "artisanal" became part of the foodie vocabulary.) His recipe would probably horrify today's acolytes of low-fat, no-carb eating, but we loved it. It's not exactly the same, but I think Daddy's spaghetti must be why I like spaghetti Bolognese so much to this day.

It wasn't just Daddy. His cousin Louise was an incredible cook. When the *Ebony* Fashion Fair whirled into town each year, Louise insisted on feeding the show's cast and crew. We kids got to be plate runners and drink-order takers. Louise's husband, who everybody called Brother, and Daddy would tend bar, cracking jokes with the models while they ate platefuls of her super-rich seafood casserole: scallops, shrimp, and crab tossed with egg noodles in a mild cheese sauce till the whole thing bubbled and was beautifully browned. ("Those girls are skinny," Daddy would marvel, "but they sure can eat!")

A couple of years ago, I called Audrey Smaltz, the statuesque diva who was the show's announcer, for a story I was working on. When I finished the official part, I told her we'd actually met, years and years ago, at Louise's house during the after-show dinner. Smaltz's warmth flooded through the phone: "Oh! We *loved* Mrs. Robinson! We *so* looked forward to going to her home when we were on the road! She fed us like we were *royalty*!"

Louise had the Feeding Gene too.

When I went off to college, near Boston, home was only a few hours away. I'd come back sometimes on the weekend and often brought friends who lived too far away to visit their parents. Now that I've had the feed-the-masses experience with my own son's gaggle of college friends, I get how expensive feeding four or five extra postadolescents can be. My parents were always glad to make a pot of spaghetti or chili. "They are always welcome here." By example, they taught me that you don't have to have a lot or a lot of fancy food to make people happy and grateful to sit at your table.

So I can't help but have the Feeding Gene. My junior and senior years in college, five of us lived in a tower, in five separate rooms with campus-wide views, our own bathroom (such luxury—no sharing with a hallway of people!), and a small kitchen. We didn't cook a lot, since the dorm had its own dining room. But sometimes when we didn't want an institutional meal, we'd cook. I remember lucking up on a bunch of shrimp one fall weekend, and after shelling them, I sautéed a handful of onions and some chopped garlic, added a couple of cans of chopped tomatoes, and finally, the shrimp. We served it over plain boiled rice and offered bowls of it to guys who'd come to visit for the afternoon. They'd brought along two Senegalese students. "Is it okay?" I asked one, as he spooned up. He looked at me with total seriousness and replied, "Tastes like home." Those three words told me he missed home a lot, and I was so happy to have brought him closer for those few minutes.

At one point several decades ago, family-close friends had moved from New York to a big country house on Boston's South Shore. They asked me to come for Thanksgiving, knowing I was freshly separated from my then-husband and feeling a little unmoored. They decided that the Thanksgiving table should be a true welcome table and also invited several other people who were at loose ends.

We cooked and cooked: a huge roast turkey, a recipe from our bible, *Gourmet*, that contained chopped oysters and crumbled sausage; collard greens and string beans and black-eyed peas; big fluffy bowls of rice *and* bowls of mashed potatoes with butter. I think there was also a ham. And bowls filled with homemade cranberry relish. There were pies and at least one cake and a big vat of vanilla ice cream for people who couldn't countenance pie *not* à la mode. The guests were a crazy quilt of people who couldn't get away or didn't want to: doctors and reporters who were on-call; other divorce refugees; an exchange student from Japan who'd never seen half the food on the table and who ate it all and then had seconds. Old friends from far away who came to reconnect after many years. We just kept putting plates on the table and whoever came was fed.

In subsequent years, that free-for-all Thanksgiving became a tradition: Original guests returned and brought others with them. The divorced (including me) remarried and eventually brought their children. The houses kept changing (the Boston couple moved to California and continued the tradition there); the guest list kept expanding (at one point, there were an insane forty people to feed), and still there were enough plates for everyone. The hosts' expanding table had expanded to the absolute limit, and the young people ended up, as they always do, at a separate table in the kitchen, but everyone had a plate and everyone was fed.

The Thanksgiving idyll ended, eventually; the Boston couple we thought would be married forever broke up. People regrouped and made their own, smaller Thanksgivings. After a few years, the rhythm picked up again. At my house, we might have between eight and a dozen people. Some are, like the original guests, at loose ends. There are always seconds, even thirds, for whomever wants them. And a plate of leftovers to take home. We run the dishwasher two or three times and hand-wash the stemware and smile about what a nice evening it was. (And there is always pie for breakfast because . . . Thanksgiving.)

During the rest of the year, we often have guests—friends, friends of friends—come for a visit and stay for a meal. It's frequently impromptu and hardly ever fancy. There's always something to turn into dinner: a couple jars of marinara, pasta, or maybe some eggs and whatever veg is in season. An omelet *aux fines herbes* or grilled cheese with pulled barbequed chicken. Or we sauté some ground turkey and make chili or tacos, and then we put some more plates on the table.

If you can claim a Feeding Gene by marriage, then I guess I get it from my in-laws too. Jay and Cee both had Louisiana roots, and it showed every year: They were famous for a huge dinner they'd have the week before Christmas. They invited plenty of family, but also former coworkers, people who had been in the service with them (like Daddy, Jay was an army vet; Cee had been a WAAC), and old friends and neighbors. Jay always made a potent eggnog, which would be topped with whipped cream, chilled, and then poured into Cee's punch bowl, a big cut-glass one she'd inherited from Jay's mother (and which she passed on to me). Cee's sisters, Alice and Stella, would take turns serving gumbo from an electric pot that kept it at the right temperature and didn't overcook the shrimp. For a second course (and in deference to guests who couldn't or didn't eat sea-food), there would be a sliced ham, potato salad, green salad, and bowls of vegetables. Everyone had what Jay called Totin' Privileges: You were encouraged to make a plate or fill a plastic container and tote something home. "If you leave here hungry," he'd warn us, "it's your own fault . . ." Now my husband says that to our guests.

The people who transmitted the Feeding Gene to us are no longer with us. My grandparents have been gone for decades now. Daddy too. Jay died several years ago, and Cee just before Christmas. And Mother shortly after the New Year began last year. We miss each of them and remember them in many ways—including through how we cook and care for our guests. At the repast following Mother's memorial service, the food was catered—pretty and very good—but the desserts were astonishing. In an extraordinarily generous gesture, several cousins offered to make the dozens and dozens of sweets for a church full of guests as a tribute to Mother, who loved her some dessert. Lada made brownies, one of Mother's favorite desserts, and caramel cake. Her daughter-in-law Daisy made small red-velvet cupcakes from the recipe Mother had given her years earlier (Daisy's preschool son, Nico, helped frost them). Lada's other daughter-in-law Sondra worked with Lada's sister Fleur to make rich, tangy lemon bars. It was a sweet ending to a bittersweet day, and proof positive that the Feeding Gene will continue in my family long after I've left the earth. Which is as it should be.

## ACKNOWLEDGMENTS

The idea for this project showed up and knocked me over one day, and my immediate certainty about the need to do it was unimpeded by having no anthologizing experience or previous desire to undertake such a thing. Fortunately, many, many people helped me along the way. Thanks go to my Anthology Think Tank, comprised of Cathi Hanauer, Marcia Aldrich, Hattie Fletcher, Veronica Chambers, Will Schwalbe, and Proposal Genie Lizzie Skurnick. Thanks to sounding boards John Howard, Daniel Mendelsohn, and M'Balia Singley. Thanks to the collegial generosity of Julia Bloch, which led to essential support from Christin Molisani, which was thanks to the University of Pennsylvania's Bassini Writing Apprenticeships Program. Another windfall of institutional support came from the amazing Civitella Ranieri Foundation, where I learned from artist James Casabere the importance of "expanding my practice."

Agent-for-life Geri Thoma, with assistance from Andrea Morrison, found the perfect home for this collection in the hands of Alicia Christensen at University of Nebraska Press—a press that publishes books that remind us of why we love books. Along with Alicia, many hands at UNP shepherded this manuscript through the process with care and diligence, including those of Emily Wendell, Rosemary Sekora, Anna Weir, Nathan Putens, Leif Milliken, Elizabeth Zaleski, and Julie Kimmel.

Finally, *finally*, my thanks go to the twenty-five contributors to this volume, the talented and wise friends, colleagues, and complete strangers who said yes.

# CONTRIBUTORS

**KAREN GRIGSBY BATES** is a correspondent for NPR's Code Switch team, which covers issues that involve race, ethnicity, and identity. In her spare time she writes novels (*Plain Brown Wrapper* and *Chosen People*) and is coauthor, with Karen Elyse Hudson, of the best-selling etiquette book *Basic Black: Home Training for Modern Times*. She lives in Los Angeles with her husband, son, and two dogs. (All are male with healthy appetites, so there are rarely leftovers.) She's currently working on a novel about black college life in the 1970s.

**S. BEAR BERGMAN** is a writer, storyteller, educator, activist, and the founder and publisher of Flamingo Rampant, which makes feminist, culturally diverse children's picture books about LGBT2Q+ kids and families. He writes creative nonfiction for grown-ups, fiction for children, resolutely factual features for various publications, the advice column Asking Bear, and he was the coeditor, with Kate Bornstein, of *Gender Outlaws: The Next Generation*. These days he spends most of his time making trans cultural competency interventions any way he can and trying to avoid stepping on Legos.

TWITTER: @sbearbergman

WEBSITE: sbearbergman.com

**LELAND CHEUK**, a MacDowell Colony and Hawthornden Castle fellow, is the author of the story collection *Letters from Dinosaurs* and the novel *The Misadventures of Sulliver Pong*. His newest novel *No Good Very Bad Asian* is forthcoming from C&R Press in 2019. He lives in Brooklyn.

TWITTER: @lcheuk

WEBSITE: lelandcheuk.com

**KATE CARROLL DE GUTES** lives in Portland, Oregon. In the evenings, she sits at her great-grandparents' quarter-sawn oak table and writes longhand about grief, the drama of dating at midlife, riding bikes, and the joys and challenges of authentic living. Kate is the author of two memoirs, *Objects in Mirror Are Closer Than They Appear* and *The Authenticity Experiment: Lessons from the Best and Worst Year of My Life*. She is a recipient of a Lambda Literary Award, an Oregon Book Award, an Independent Publishing Award, and she has received fellowships from the Anderson Center, Centrum, and the Virginia Center for the Creative Arts.

TWITTER: @kcdegutes

WEBSITE: katecarrolldegutes.com

**LOLIS ERIC ELIE** has written for newspapers (*Times-Picayune*, *Atlanta Journal-Constitution*), for magazines (*The Oxford American*, *The Bitter Southerner*, *The Art of Eating*, *Gourmet*, *Bon Appetit*), and for television (*Treme*, *Greenleaf*, *The Man in the High Castle*). But mostly, he writes for food. His essay, "America's Greatest Hits," was included in *Best African American Essays: 2009*. Born and raised in New Orleans, he currently divides his time between the Crescent City and Los Angeles.

TWITTER: @LolisEricElie

WEBSITE: LolisEricElie.com

**CAROLYN FERRELL** is the author of the short-story collection *Don't Erase Me*, awarded the Art Seidenbaum Award of the *Los Angeles Times* Book Prize, the John C. Zachiris Award given by *Ploughshares*, and the Quality Paperback Book Prize for First Fiction. Her stories have been anthologized in *Best American Short Stories 2018*; *The Best American Short Stories of the Century*; *Giant Steps: The New Generation of African American Writers*; *The Blue Light Corner: Black Women Writing on Passion, Sex, and Romantic Love*; and *Children of the Night: The Best Short Stories by Black Writers, 1967 to the Present*. Ferrell has received grants from the Fulbright Association, German Academic Exchange (DAAD), and the National Endowment for the Arts. She teaches at Sarah Lawrence College.

**JOHN FREEMAN** is the award-winning editor of the literary biannual *Freeman's*. His books include *The Tyranny of Email*, *How to Read a Novelist*, and *Apathy Body Citizen*, as well as two books of poems, *Maps* and *The Park*. He has assembled two anthologies of new writing on inequality, *Tales of Two Cities* and *Tales of*

*Two Americas*. His work has appeared in *The New Yorker*, *The Paris Review*, and the *New York Times* and been translated into twenty-two languages. Currently executive editor of the Literary Hub, he lives in New York where he is artist in residence at NYU.

TWITTER: @FreemanReads

**LAUREN GRODSTEIN** is the author of four novels, including *Our Short History* and *A Friend of the Family*. She directs the MFA program at Rutgers-Camden.

TWITTER: @laurengrodstein

WEBSITE: laurengrodstein.com

**JANE HAMILTON**'s novels have won literary prizes, been made into films, been international best-sellers, and two of them, *The Book of Ruth* and *A Map of The World*, were selections of Oprah's Book Club. Her nonfiction has appeared in the *New York Times*, the *Washington Post*, *Allure*, *Oprah Magazine*, *Elle*, and various anthologies. She's married to an apple farmer and lives in Wisconsin.

WEBSITE: janehamiltonbooks.com

**SUSAN ITO** is the author of *The Mouse Room* and editor of the literary anthology *A Ghost at Heart's Edge: Stories and Poems of Adoption*. She has been a columnist and editor at *Literary Mama*, and her work has appeared in *Growing Up Asian American*, *Choice*, *Hip Mama*, *Hyphen*, *Catapult*, and *The Bellevue Literary Review*. She has performed her solo show, *The Ice Cream Gene*, around the United States. She cowrote the theatrical anthology *Untold*, stories of reproductive stigma. She teaches at Mills College, BayPath University, and the San Francisco Writers' Grotto.

TWITTER: @thesusanito

WEBSITE: thesusanito.com

**MAT JOHNSON** is the author of the novels *Loving Day*, *Pym*, *Drop*, and *Hunting in Harlem*, the nonfiction novella *The Great Negro Plot*, and the comic books *Incognegro* and *Dark Rain*. He is a recipient of the American Book Award, the United States Artist James Baldwin Fellowship, the Hurston/Wright Legacy Award, a Barnes & Noble Discover Great New Writers selection, and the John Dos Passos Prize for Literature. Johnson is a professor at the University of Oregon.

TWITTER: @mat_johnson

WEBSITE: matjohnson.info

**DONNA MASINI** is the author of three books of poems—*4:30 Movie*, *Turning to Fiction*, *That Kind of Danger*—and a novel, *About Yvonne*. Her work has appeared in journals and anthologies including *Poetry*, *Ploughshares*, *The American Poetry Review*, *The Paris Review*, *The Pushcart Prize*, and *The Best American Poetry 2015*. A recipient of grants from the National Endowment for the Arts and the New York Foundation for the Arts, she teaches in the MFA Creative Writing program at Hunter College.

TWITTER: @DonnaMasini

WEBSITE: donnamasini.com

**DANIEL MENDELSOHN** is a longtime contributor to *The New Yorker* and *New York Review of Books* and has been a columnist for BBC Culture, *New York*, *Harper's*, and the *New York Times Book Review*. His memoirs include *An Odyssey: A Father, a Son, and an Epic*, named a Best Book of the Year by NPR, *Library Journal*, *Kirkus*, and *Newsday*; the international bestseller *The Lost: A Search for Six of Six Million*; and *The Elusive Embrace: Desire and the Riddle of Identity*, a *Los Angeles Times* Best Book of the Year. He is also the author of two collections of essays and a translation, with commentary, of the complete poems of Constantine Cavafy. He teaches literature at Bard College.

TWITTER: @DanielMendelsohn

WEBSITE: danielmendelsohn.com

**MARC MEWSHAW** graduated cum laude from Princeton and holds an MFA in creative writing from NYU. His fiction has appeared in *Lost Magazine*, *The New Guard*, and *Descant*, among others. A 2008 Director's Guest at Civitella Ranieri Foundation, he was awarded the Solares Hill short-story prize and nominated for Best New American Voices in 2005. His travel journalism and essays have appeared in the *New York Times*, the *Boston Globe*, *The Telegraph*, Atlantic.com, and *The Millions*, among others.

**LAURA MILLER**, a journalist and critic living in New York, is books and culture columnist for *Slate*. She is a cofounder of Salon.com, where she worked for twenty years. Her work has appeared in *The New Yorker*, *Harper's*, the *Guardian*, and the *New York Times Book Review*, where she wrote the column The Last Word. She is the author of *The Magician's Book: A Skeptic's Adventures in Narnia* and editor of the *The Salon.com Reader's Guide to Contemporary Authors*.

TWITTER: @magiciansbook

WEBSITE: lauramiller.org

**KYOKO MORI** is the author of three nonfiction books (*The Dream of Water, Polite Lies, Yarn*) and four novels (*Shizuko's Daughter, One Bird, Stone Field, True Arrow, Barn Cat*). Her stories and essays have appeared in *Harvard Review, Fourth Genre, Ploughshares*, the *American Scholar, Conjunctions, The Best American Essays*, and other journals and anthologies. She teaches in George Mason University's MFA Program in Creative Writing and Lesley University's Low-Residency MFA Program. Kyoko lives in Washington DC with her two cats, Miles and Jackson.

WEBSITE: kyokomori.com

**ANN PATCHETT** is the author of seven novels: *The Patron Saint of Liars, Taft, The Magician's Assistant, Bel Canto, Run, State of Wonder*, and *Commonwealth*. She was the editor of *Best American Short Stories, 2006*. She has written three books of nonfiction—*Truth and Beauty*, about her friendship with the writer Lucy Grealy, *What Now?* an expansion of her graduation address at Sarah Lawrence College, and *This Is the Story of a Happy Marriage*, a collection of essays examining the theme of commitment—and a picture book. A graduate of Sarah Lawrence College and the Iowa Writer's Workshop, Patchett has been the recipient of numerous awards and fellowships, including England's Orange Prize, the PEN/Faulkner Award, the Book Sense Book of the Year, a Guggenheim Fellowship, and the *Chicago Tribune*'s Heartland Prize. She is the co-owner of Parnassus Books in Nashville, Tennessee.

BLOG: parnassusmusing.net/category/anns-blog/

WEBSITE: annpatchett.com

**DANA PRESCOTT** has lived and worked in Italy for over thirty years. She is the author of *Around Rome with Kids* and is editor of the anthology *Feathers from the Angel's Wing*, a collection of poets' responses to the paintings of Piero Della Francesca. She has written travel essays for the *Christian Science Monitor*, the *Seattle Times*, the *Washington Post*, and others. Her poems have been published in the *Bennington Review* and the *Journal of Poetic Research*. She has served as director for the European Honors Program of the Rhode Island School of Design, as Andrew Heiskell arts director at the American Academy in Rome, and she is now the executive director of the Civitella Ranieri Foundation in Umbria. She has taught in the Rome programs of Cornell University, Temple University, and the University of Washington, among others.

**LIZZIE SKURNICK** is the author of *That Should Be Word* and *Shelf Discovery: The Teen Classics We Never Stopped Reading*. The founding editor of the young adult imprint Lizzie Skurnick Books, she teaches at New York University.

TWITTER: @lizzieskurnick

WEBSITE: lizzieskurnick.com

**AVI STEINBERG** has written two books of narrative nonfiction. His most recent, *The Lost Book of Mormon*, was long-listed for the Thurber Prize for American Humor. But most people prefer his first, *Running the Books: The Adventures of an Accidental Prison Librarian*. He is a frequent contributor to the *New York Times Magazine* and the *New Yorker*'s Culture Desk.

TWITTER: @avi_steinberg

**ANGELIQUE STEVENS**'s nonfiction can be found in *The Chattahoochee Review*, *Cleaver*, *Shark Reef*, and a number of anthologies. Her essay "All the Grains of Sand" won the grand prize in the Solas Award for Best Travel Writing 2018, and her experimental essay "Spiral" was published in the anthology *Friend Follow, Text*, which was nominated by *Foreword Reviews* for Best Anthology of the Year. She holds an MFA from Bennington College and is currently writing a travel memoir about her trip to South Sudan and her experiences growing up in New York State.

TWITTER: @angelique23456

**CLIFFORD THOMPSON** received a Whiting Writers' Award for nonfiction in 2013 for *Love for Sale and Other Essays*. He is the author of the memoir *Twin of Blackness* and the novel *Signifying Nothing*. His writing has appeared in such publications as *The Best American Essays 2018*, the *Washington Post*, the *Wall Street Journal*, the *Village Voice*, the *Times Literary Supplement*, *The Threepenny Review*, *Commonweal*, *Cineaste*, and *The Los Angeles Review of Books*. For over a dozen years, he served as the editor of *Current Biography*, and he has taught creative nonfiction writing at the Bennington Writing Seminars, New York University, Columbia University, Queens College, and Sarah Lawrence College. His book *What It Is: Race, Family, and One Thinking Black Man's Blues* will be published in 2019. He lives in Brooklyn.

TWITTER: @616Clifford

WEBSITE: cliffordthompson.info

**SHUKREE HASSAN TILGHMAN** worked as an editor on *Dog the Bounty Hunter* and various other semi-ridiculous cable reality shows before coming to his senses and pursuing an MFA in screenwriting at Columbia University. Upon graduation, he continued to mine the depths of the reality-show underworld, cutting "redneck reality" and house flipping shows until he was saved by a job as a writer on the USA drama series *Satisfaction*. He went on to write on *The Vampire Diaries* and penned the pilot *Tempest*. He is currently a writer/producer on the NBC series *This Is Us*. Tilghman has produced and directed nonfiction projects, including the PBS documentary film *More Than a Month* and *The March@50*, a PBS.org documentary series about the anniversary of the 1963 March on Washington. Tilghman received a BFA in film and television from New York University.

TWITTER: @shukreehassan

SALLIE TISDALE is the author of nine books, most recently *Advice for Future Corpses (and Those Who Love Them)*. Her other books include *Talk Dirty to Me*, *Stepping Westward*, and *Women of the Way*. Her collection of essays, *Violation*, was published in 2015 by Hawthorne Books. Her work has appeared in *Harper's*, *Antioch Review*, *Conjunctions*, *Threepenny Review*, *The New Yorker*, and *Tricycle*, among other journals. Tisdale is the 2013 recipient of the Regional Arts and Culture Council Literary Fellowship. She has received a Pushcart Prize, a National Endowment for the Arts Fellowship, the James D. Phelan Literary Award, and she was a Dorothy and Arthur Shoenfeldt Distinguished Writer of the Year. Tisdale is a longtime member of PEN and teaches part-time in the writing program at Portland State University.

BLOG: http://stisdale.tumblr.com/
WEBSITE: www.sallietisdale.com

LAURA VAN DEN BERG is the author of two novels, *The Third Hotel* and *Find Me*, and the story collections *What the World Will Look Like When All the Water Leaves Us* and *The Isle of Youth*, both finalists for the Frank O'Connor International Short Story Award. Her honors include the Bard Fiction Prize, the Rosenthal Family Foundation Award from the American Academy of Arts and Letters, a Pushcart Prize, an O. Henry Award, and fellowships from the MacDowell Colony and the Civitella Ranieri Foundation. Born and raised in Florida, Laura currently lives in Cambridge, Massachusetts, where she is a Briggs-Copeland Lecturer in Fiction at Harvard University.

TWITTER: @Lvandenberg
WEBSITE: lauravandenberg.com